Riddles for Adults
flexible and challenging tasks in the fields of logic, maths, geometry and textriddles

„Probably only 2 % of the world population is able to solve this riddle." - With this saying, Einstein referred to the riddle of pure logic, known as Einstein-riddle.

Such challenges are rarely found today.

This collection of challenging tasks in the fields of logic, maths, geometry, concentration, understanding, decoding and systematic approach contrasts with the standardriddles of these days.

The riddles are designed logically and have high demands on the reader.
Sometimes, the riddles are structured in different levels of difficulty so that a scheme for solving can be developed.

Carsten Richter

Riddles for Adults
flexible and challenging tasks in the fields of logic, maths, geometry and textriddles

Carsten Richter

The German National library lists this publication in the German National bibliography; detailed bibliographic data is available on the Internet via http://dnb.dnb.de.

© 2016 Carsten Richter

Illustration: Carsten Richter

Production and publishing company: BoD – Books on Demand, Norderstedt

ISBN: 9 783 741 292 392

Contents:

Preface

1.	**Riddles of geometry**	**4-33**
1.1.	Level of difficulty: low	
1.2.	Level of difficulty: middle	
1.3.	Level of difficulty: high	
2.	**Logicals – Fix up the chaos**	**34-65**
2.1.	Level of difficulty: middle	
2.2.	Level of difficulty: high	
2.3.	Level of difficulty: very high	
3.	**Sequences of numbers**	**66-73**
3.1.	Level of difficulty: low	
3.2.	Level of difficulty: middle	
3.3.	Level of difficulty: high	
3.4.	Level of difficulty: very high	
4.	**Complete the formulae**	**74-92**
4.1.	Level of difficulty: low	
4.2.	Level of difficulty: middle	
4.3.	Level of difficulty: high	
5.	**Textriddles**	**93-112**
5.1.	The relocation	
5.2.	Timezones	
5.3.	Murder among colleagues	
5.4.	4 friends	
5.5.	Who stole the motorcycle?	

5.6.	5 people	
5.7.	6 colleagues – what they like and dislike	
5.8.	The mystery of speed	
5.9.	Burglary in the cellar at the barbecue evening	
5.10.	The age	
5.11.	3 tigers and 3 zebras	
5.12.	Workplaces	
5.13.	Chaos with the cups	
5.14.	Expenses at purchase	
5.15.	The line in the supermarket	
6.	**Miscellaneous**	**112-121**
6.1.	The most difficult riddle in the world: „The riddle of columns"	
6.2.	Text and numbers	
6.3.	Number blocks	
6.4.	Logic	
6.5.	Complete the task	
6.6.	Which city are we looking for?	
6.7.	Find the city	
6.8.	Spaceships and the light	
6.9.	The age	

Solution part   **122-158**

Preface

This collection of riddles is intended for people who are looking for special challenges. For many people, the classical standard riddles are no longer satisfying. Of course, a sudoku can be designed more difficult and can be challenging for the puzzling person, but its nothing new.
Intelligence is a result of creativity. This is the ability to develope systems and strategies for special tasks and problems. Therefore, various types of riddles are essential to ensure that mental flexibility is maintained.

To venture on a new construct of tasks, a sensible structure in the difficulty is required. If you start with the most challenging task at other riddles, you run into danger not to develope an adequate method for solution. Your mind needs training for solving the tasks. That is why, the riddles – wherever possible – are divided into several levels of difficulty.
The ability to rethink and to see problems from different perspectives is important for solving the tasks.
An additional factor is the high demand on concentration, especially in the more difficult fields. These riddles are mostly nothing for alongside, but require attention.

„Neurobics" and intelligence tests are things in which people are increasingly interested. That is a good thing, because it is a reasonable goal in life to improve your skills. It is a fact that people who are faced with many different kind of problems and their solutions, are more creative than people who solve very specialized tasks profoundly. If you look at the construction of diverse intelligence tests, – however, the question of intelligence is not finally clarified and can be extensively covered in the field of philosophy - creativity is important for success in different tasks. So, you can quite conclude from creativity to intelligence.

The riddles in this book will exhaust your creativity and call for your full concentration.
Use the solution part sparingly. If necessary, try to let another person check if your result is right. If not, puzzle further. To think about a problem intensively, requires patience which is also a trainable virtue.

An important note: Do not risk fastening onto a riddle. Put it aside for a moment and try again later. Do not think linearly, but be creative.

Good luck!

1. Riddles of geometry

Each riddle shows geometrical figures which are in relation to each other. Lengths of line segments can be solved mathematically and geometrically, due to fixed geometrical proportions.
One such length is always given. Recognizing the geometrical relations and performing the mathematical solution will give you the exact result. The drawings are not to scale.

Important notice:
1. The result always has to be accurate to two decimal places.
2. The three subchapters refer to a certain area of geometric theorems. These always stand at the end of the solution part, so you get the chance to conclude to the theorems by yourself, even if you check a result.
3. **Each interim result is rounded to 2 decimal digits. This includes also partial results in a formula.** To generate $y=2\times1.49^2$, you have to calculate $1.49^2=2.2201$, first. Afterward, you continue to calculate with the rounded value : $2.22 \times 2 = 4.44$.
Please, absolutely mind the forementioned details. Slight rounding differences exponentiate and cause deviations from the result.
4. Only the third digit is important for rounding, while the fourth is therefore irrelevant. For values greater or equal to 5, please round up.
Examples:

calculated value:	rounded value:
4.1648352	4.16
5.00213553	5.00
4.9952131	5.00
4.99493	4.99

1.1. Level of difficulty: low

1.1.1.

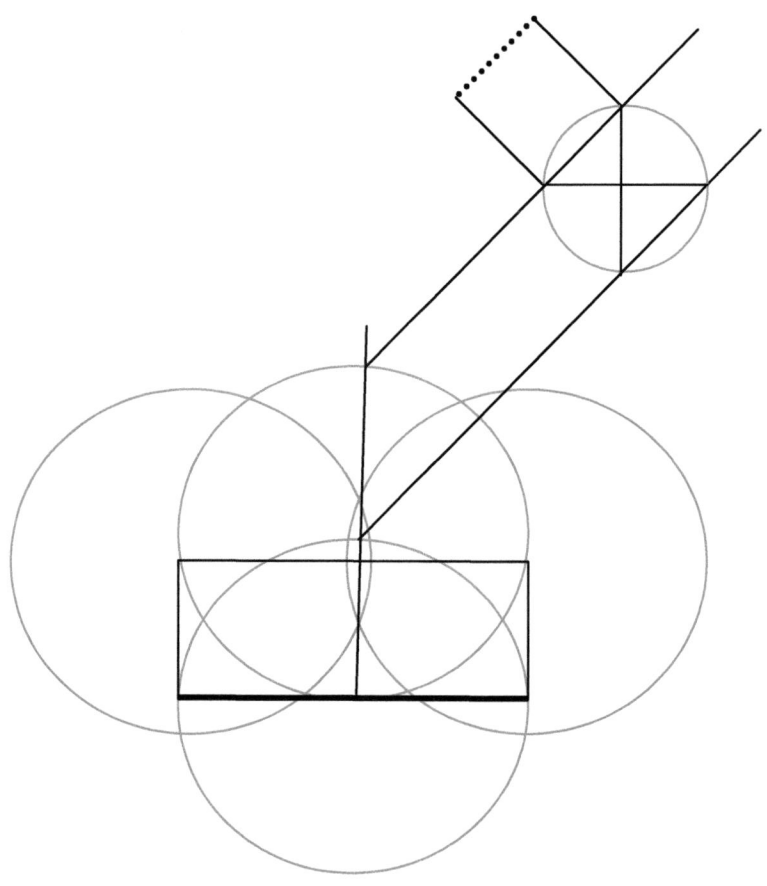

The thick line is 5.64 cm long.
How long is the dotted line?

1.1.2.

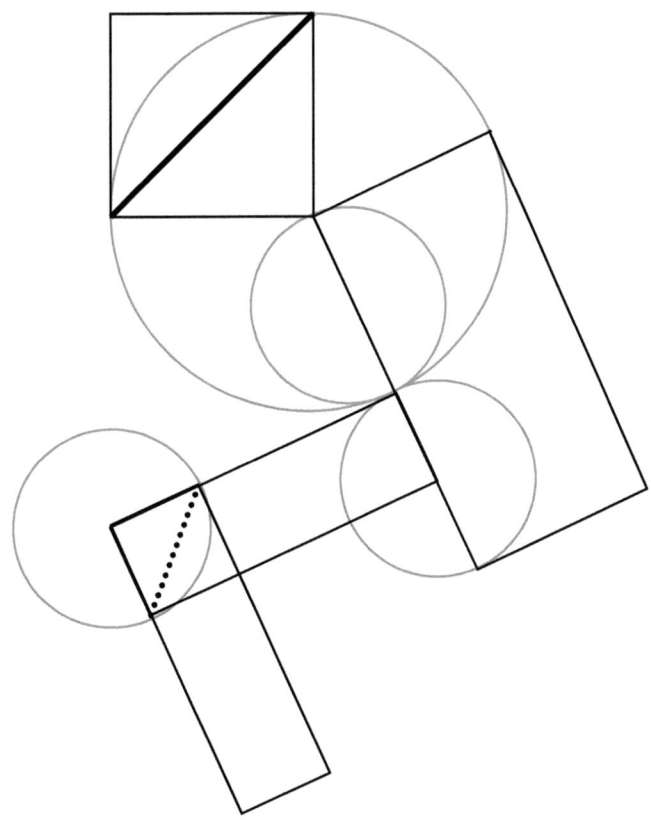

The thick line is 12.75 cm long.
How long is the dotted line?

1.1.3.

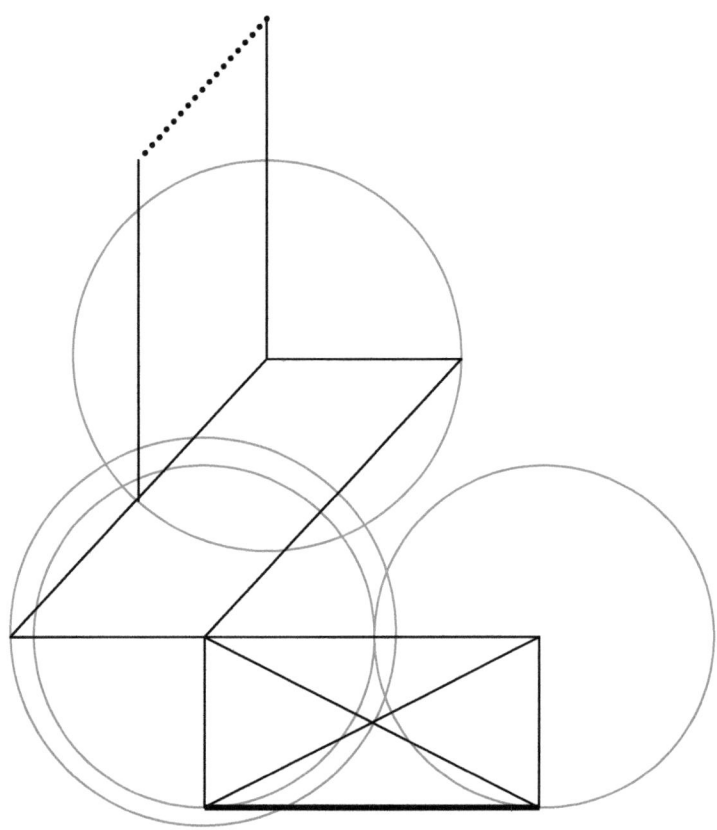

The thick line is 4.80 cm long.
How long is the dotted line?

1.1.4.

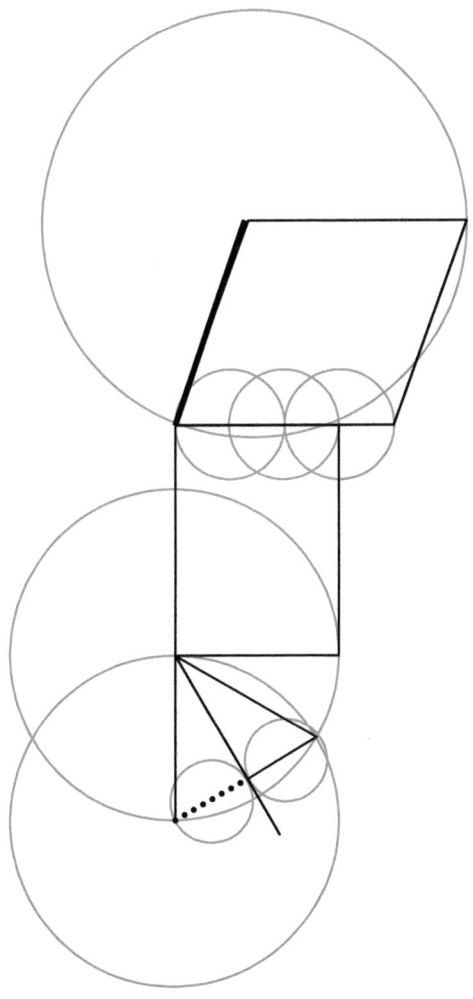

The thick line is 33.48 cm long.
How long is the dotted line?

1.1.5.

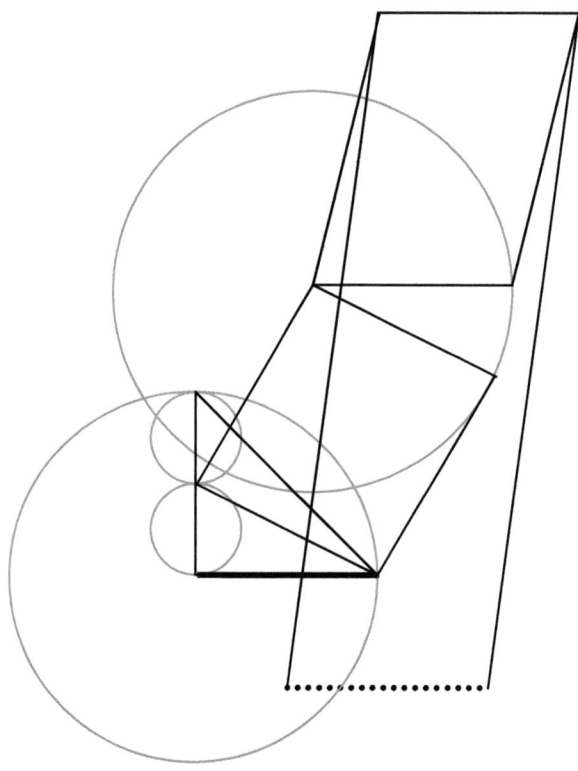

The thick line is 100.40 cm long.
How long is the dotted line?

1.1.6.

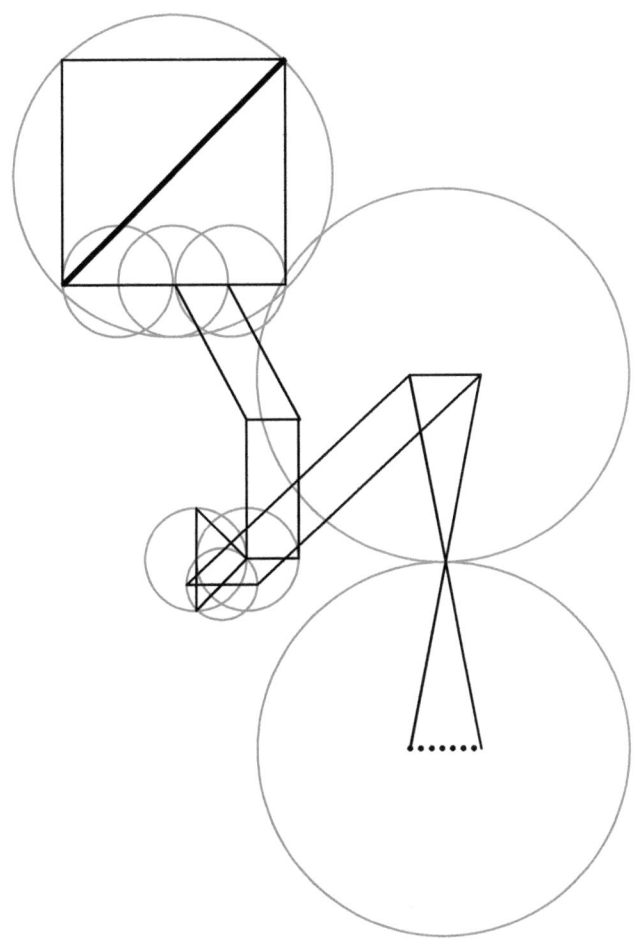

The thick line is 40 cm long.
How long is the dotted line?

1.1.7.

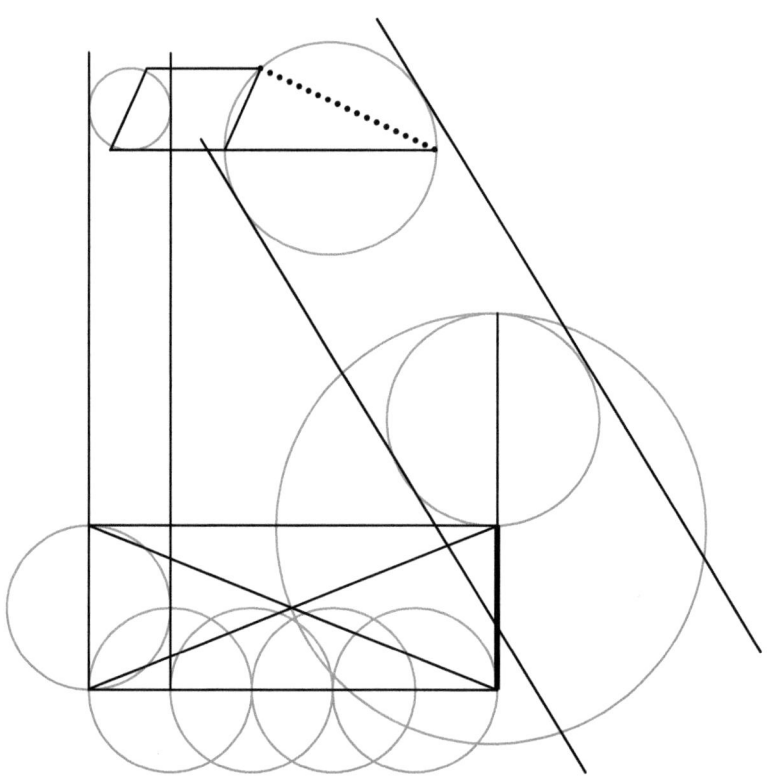

The thick line is 50.50 cm long.
How long is the dotted line?

1.1.8.

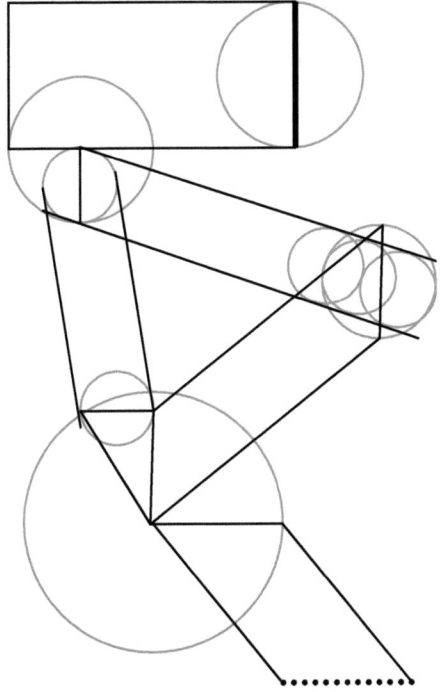

The thick line is 40.00 cm long.
How long is the dotted line?

1.1.9.

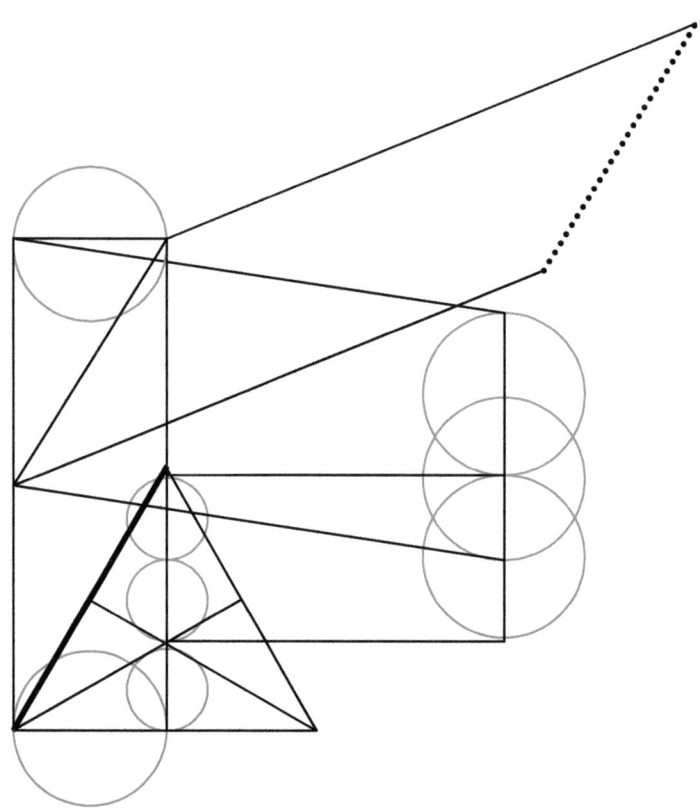

The thick line is 26.40 cm long.
How long is the dotted line?

1.1.10.

The thick line is 4.00 cm long.
How long is the dotted line?

1.2. Level of difficulty: middle

1.2.1.

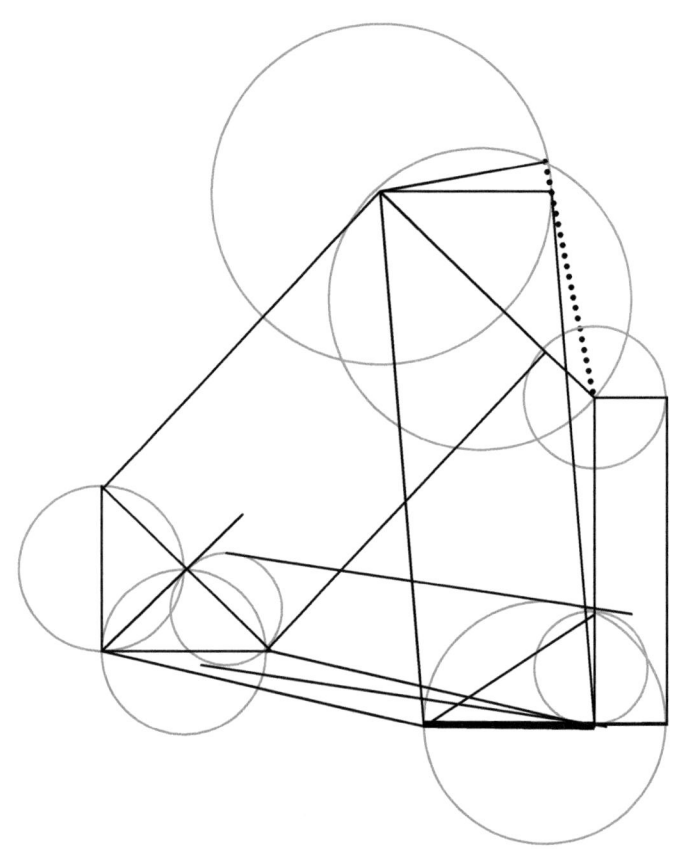

The thick line is 7.83 cm long.
How long is the dotted line?

1.2.2.

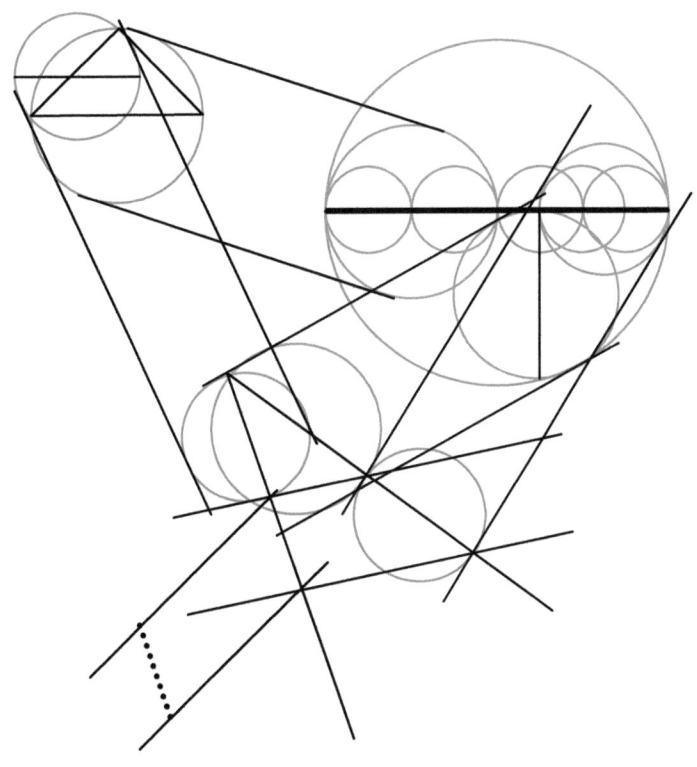

The thick line is 16.80 cm long.
How long is the dotted line?

1.2.3.

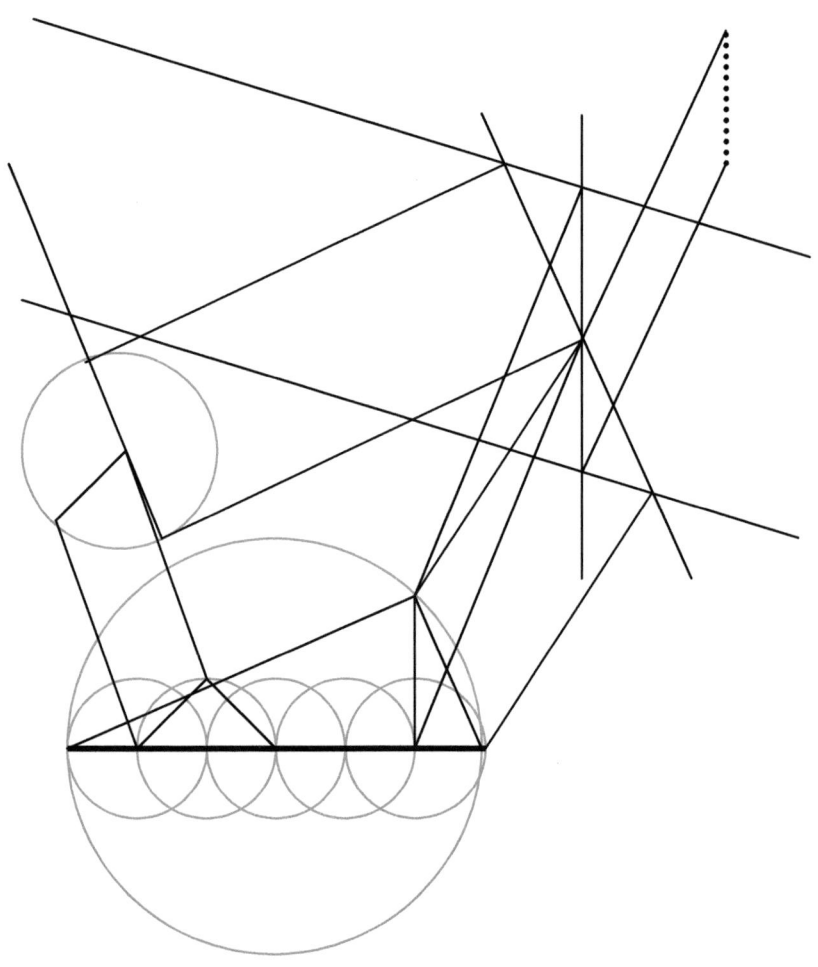

The thick line is 2.20 cm long.
How long is the dotted line?

1.2.4.

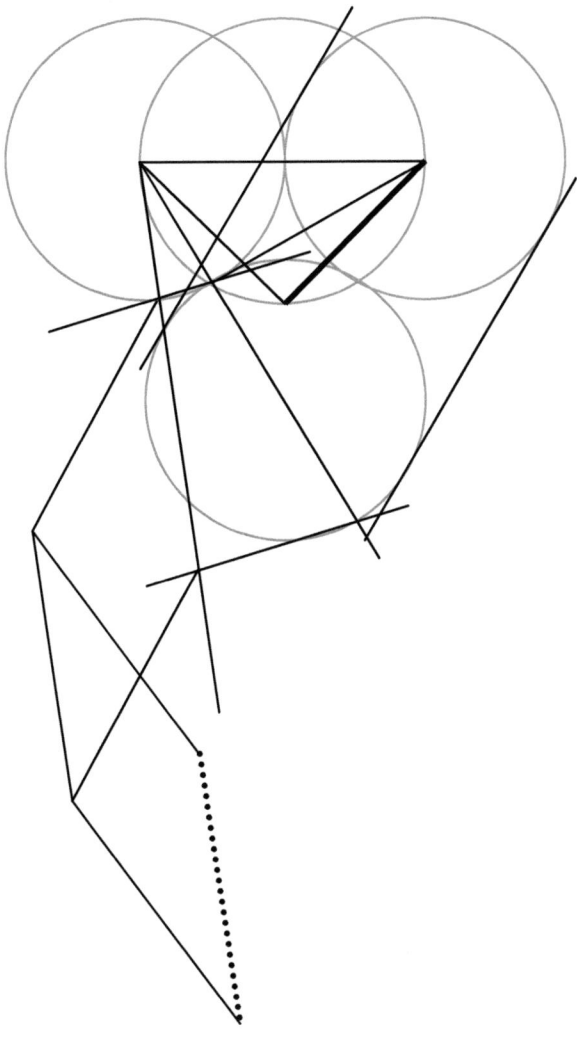

The thick line is 12.48 cm long.
How long is the dotted line?

1.2.5.

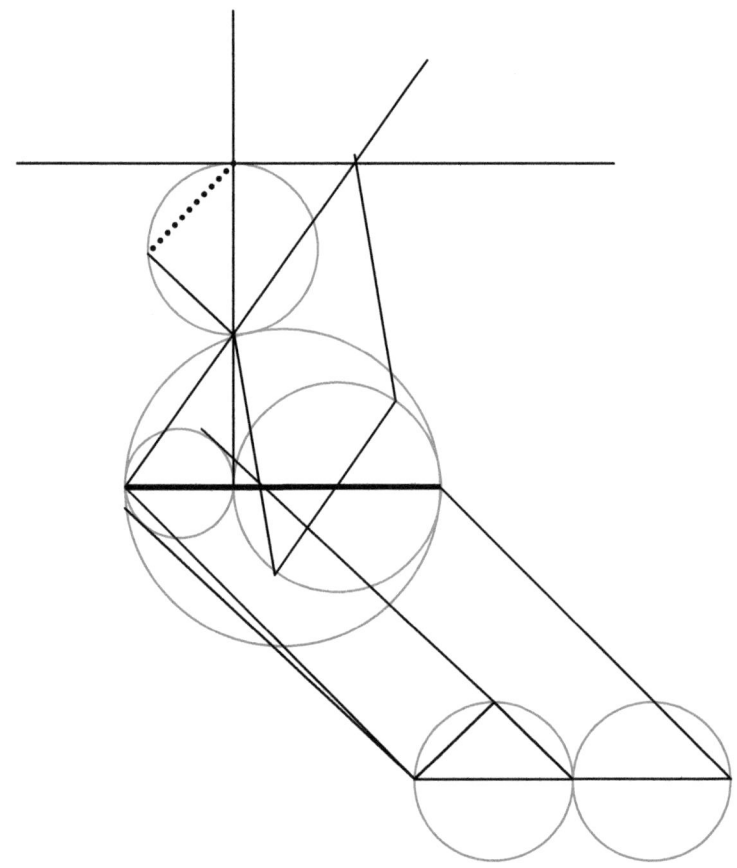

The thick line is 13.25 cm long.
How long is the dotted line?

1.2.6.

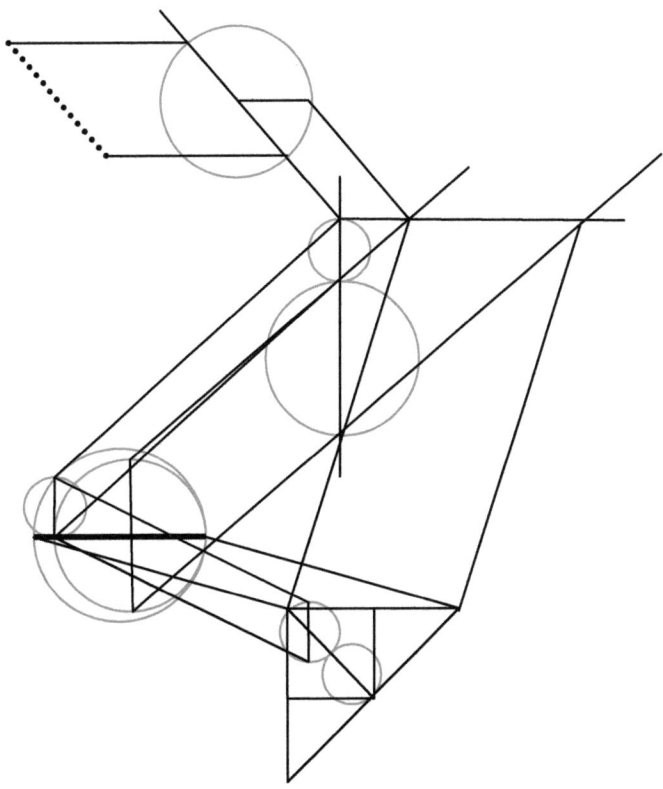

The thick line is 8.28 cm long.
How long is the dotted line?

1.2.7.

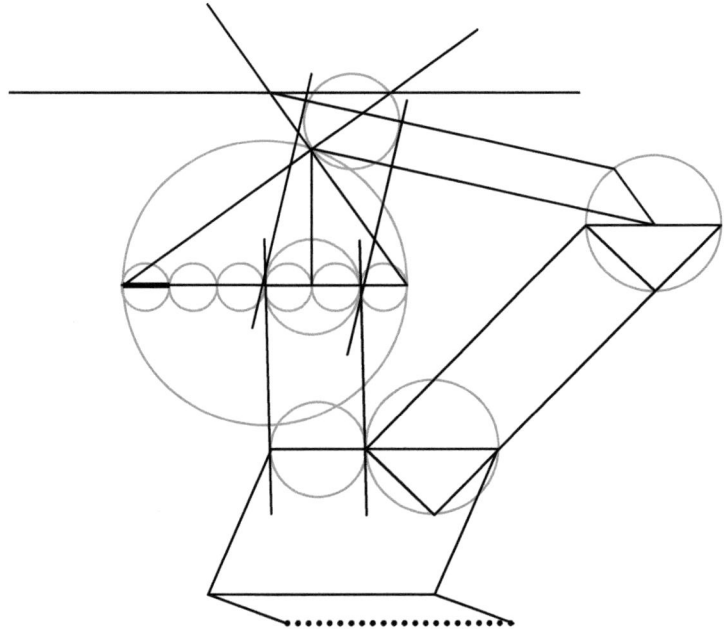

The thick line is 1.2 cm long.
How long is the dotted line?

1.2.8.

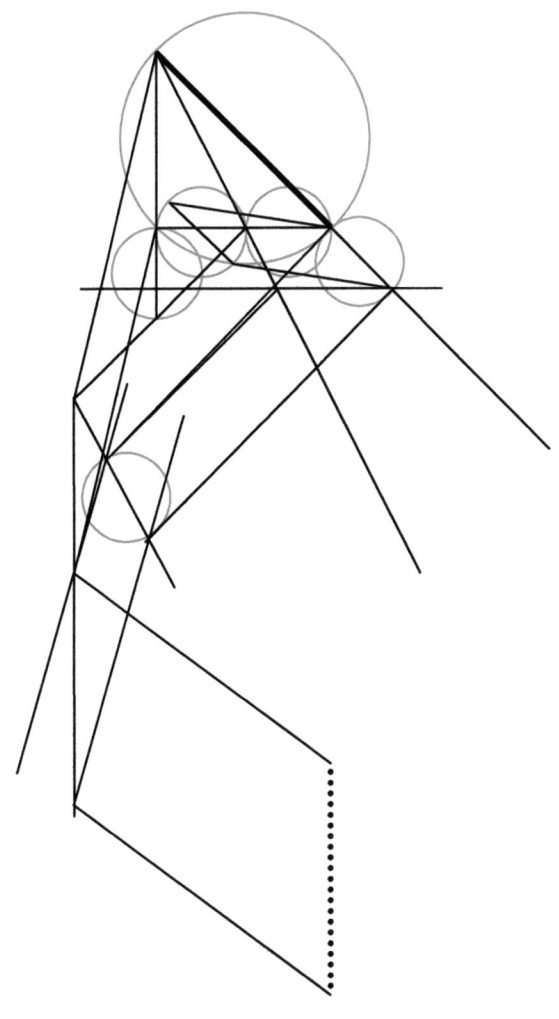

The thick line is 10.40 cm long.
How long is the dotted line?

1.2.9.

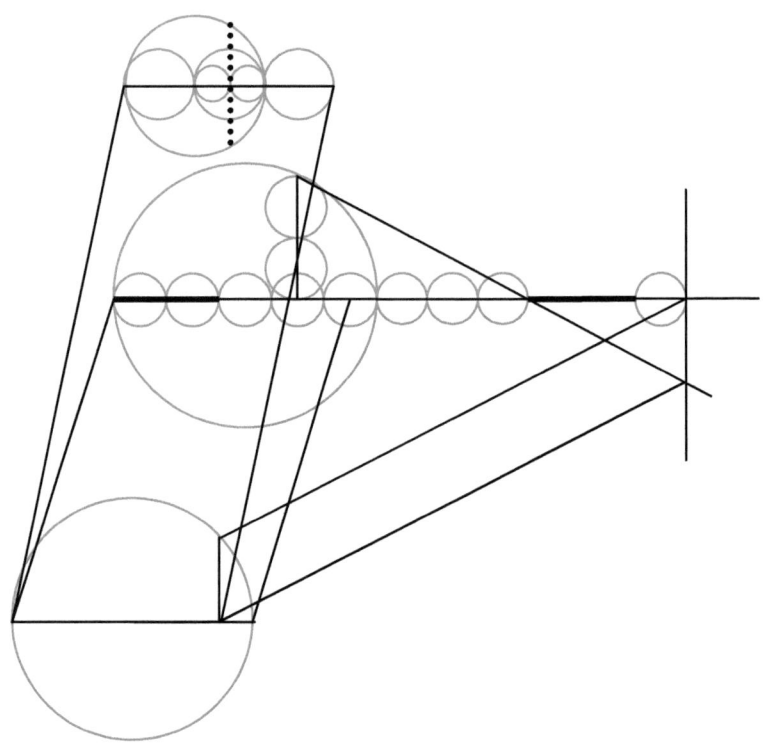

The thick line is 4.60 cm long.
How long is the dotted line?

1.2.10.

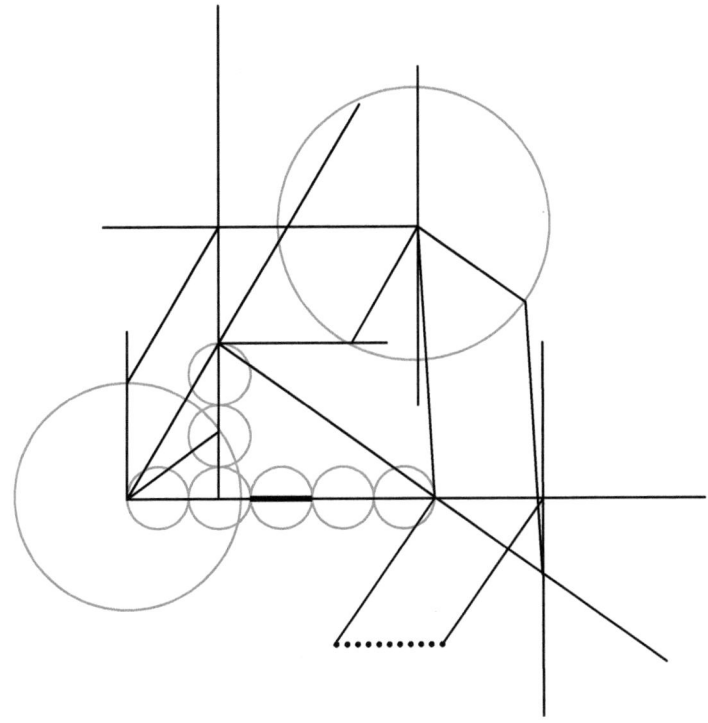

The thick line is 4.00 cm long.
How long is the dotted line?

1.3. Level of difficulty: high
1.3.1.

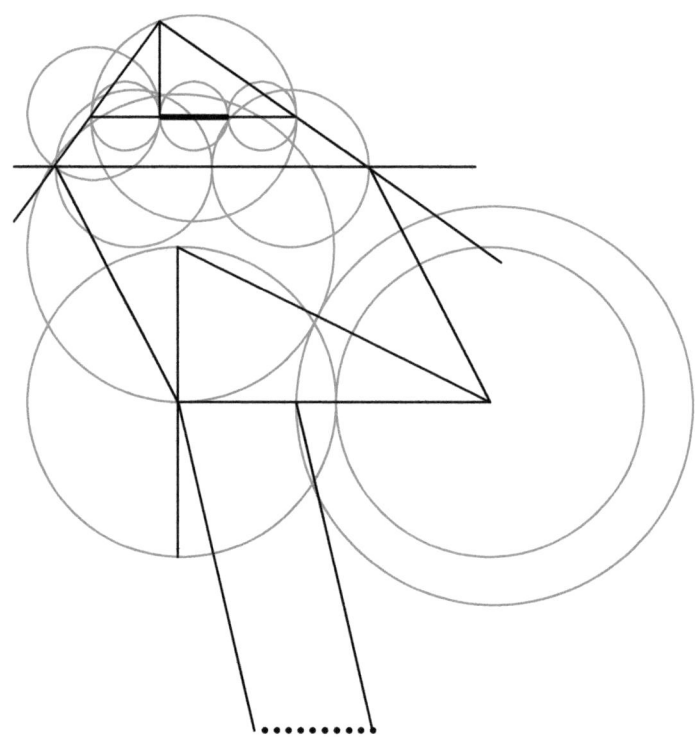

The thick line is 2.8 cm long.
How long is the dotted line?

1.3.2.

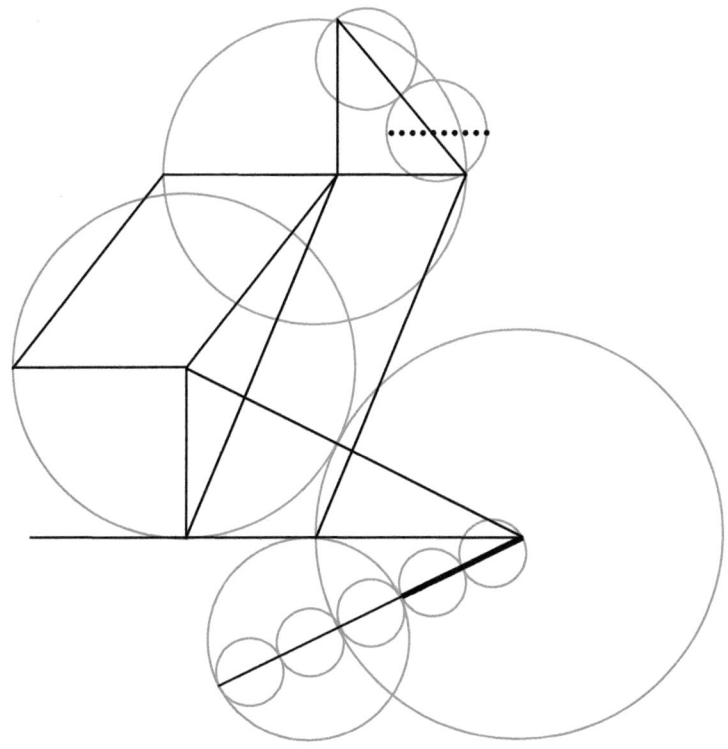

The thick line is 5.12 cm long.
How long is the dotted line?

1.3.3.

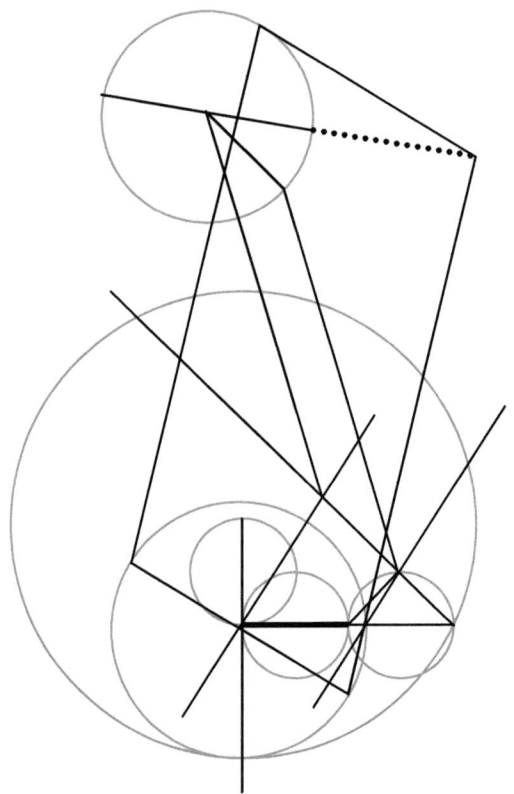

The thick line is 6 cm long.
How long is the dotted line?

1.3.4.

The thick line is 14 cm long.
How long is the dotted line?

1.3.5.

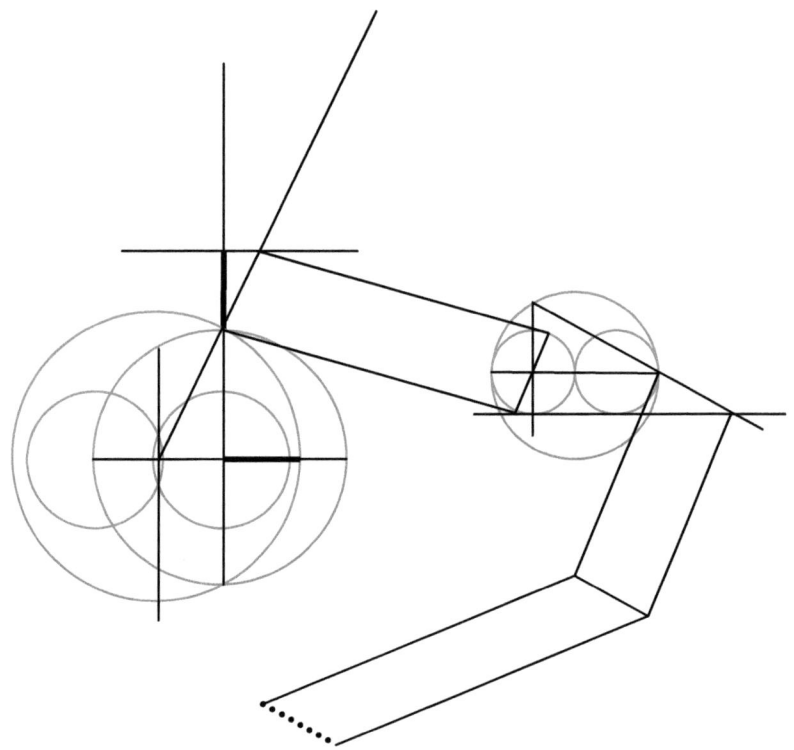

The thick lines are 9 cm long.
How long is the dotted line?

1.3.6.

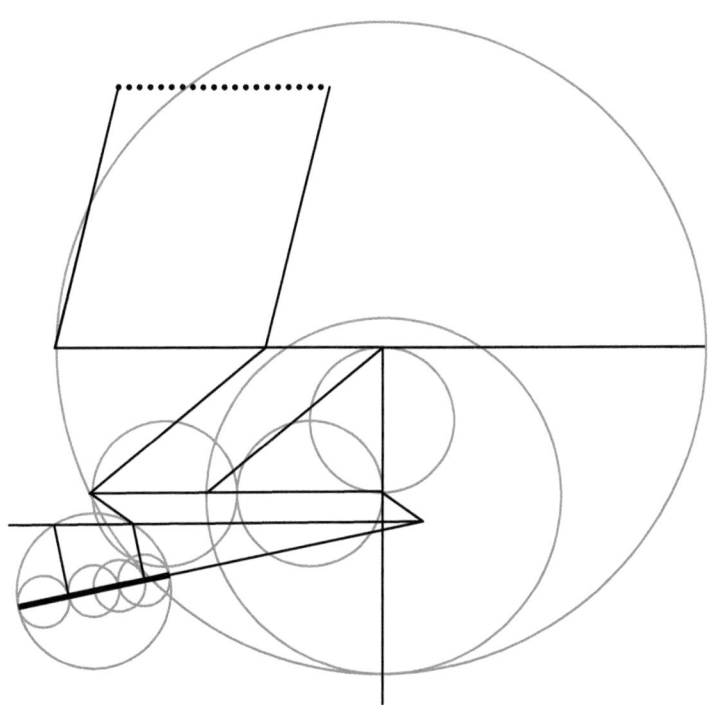

The thick line is 12 cm long.
How long is the dotted line?

1.3.7.

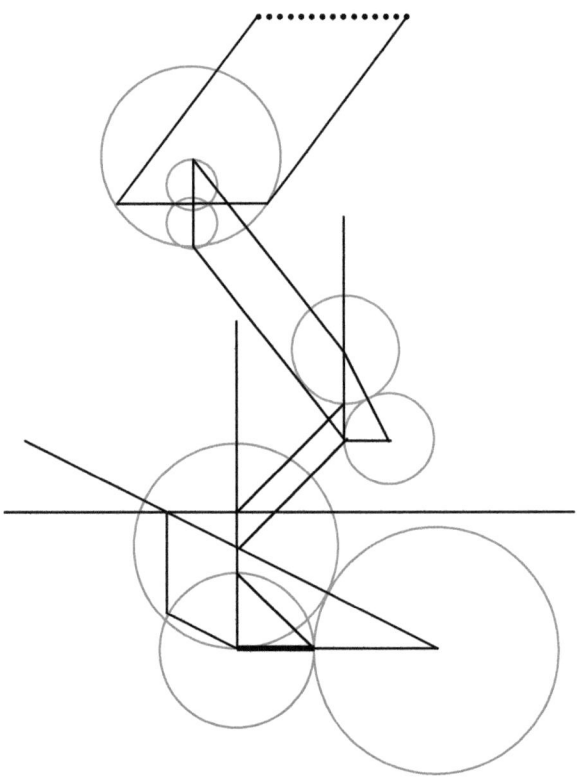

—————

The thick line is 12 cm long.
How long is the dotted line?

1.3.8.

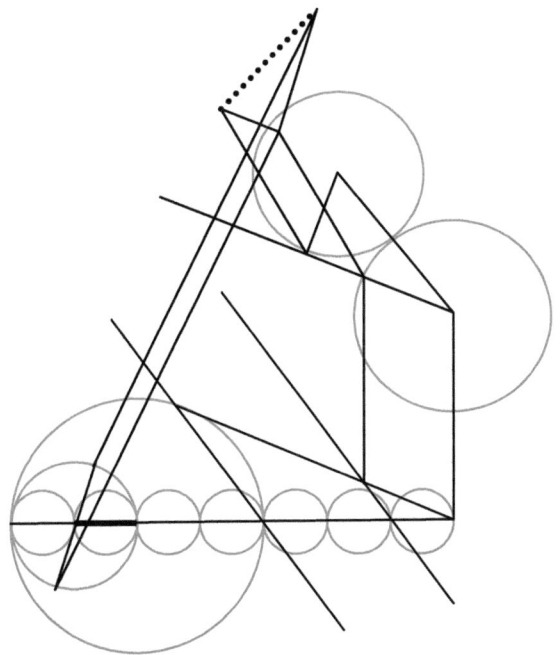

———

The thick line is 2.50 cm long.
How long is the dotted line?

1.3.9.

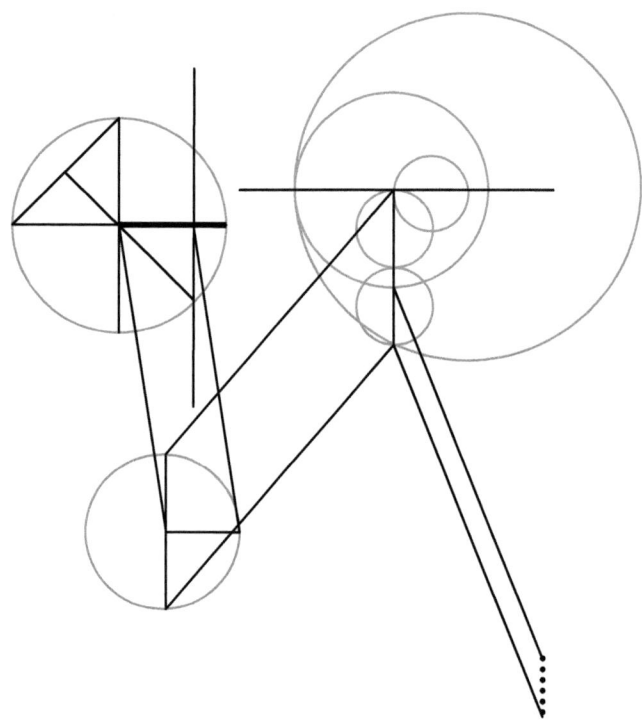

The thick line is 4.8 cm long.
How long is the dotted line?

1.3.10.

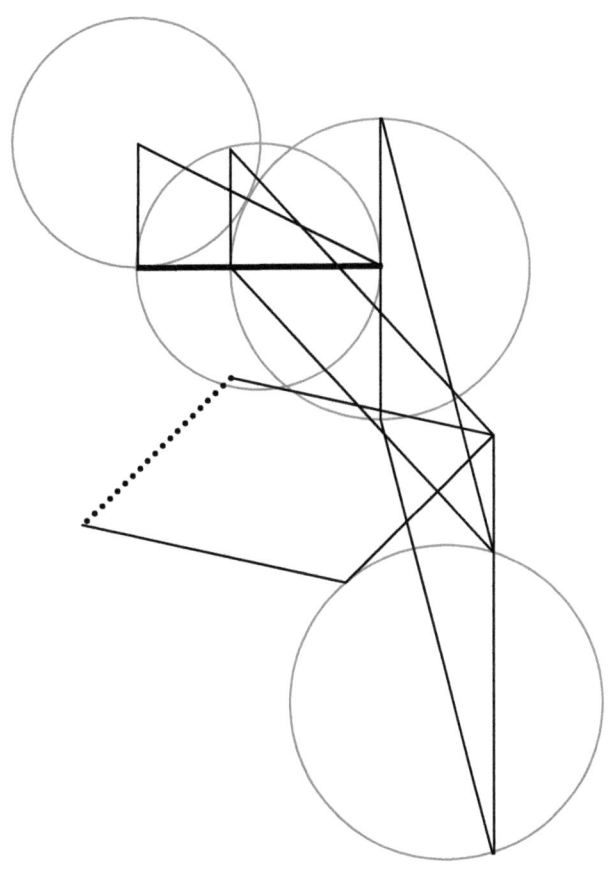

The thick line is 24.2 cm long.
How long is the dotted line?

2. Logicals – Fix up the chaos

In each riddle of that kind, the characteristics of a certain number of houses are given in relation with each other.
The number of houses, as well as the number and kind of characteristics are described shortly. No characteristic appears twice. Information about left and right is referred to the reader's perspective.

Attention, concentration and systematical thinking are important for these riddles.

The solution part partially contains hints if special approaches are appropriate. It is useful to do the riddles chronologically, as hints for new problems are only given once at the first occurrence.

2.1. Level of difficulty: middle

2.1.1. There are 4 houses. For each house there is information about the number of residents, the house´s color and the car brand.

What color is the house with 3 people?

1. 5 people live in the Peugeot driver´s house.
2. The leftmost house has the most residents.
3. A green house is next to the house of the VW driver.
4. Only 2 people live in the house which is to the right of the white house.
5. Next to the Mazda driver there lives a Peugeot driver.
6. The Mazda driver lives in the yellow house.
7. 2 people live in the yellow house.
8. Next to the white house there lives an Audi driver.
9. 6 people live in the brown house.
10 To the left of the Audi driver there is a brown house.

2.1.2. There are 4 houses. For each house there is information about the number of steps in the doorway, the number of windows and the number of children.

How many windows does the house with one child have?

1. One house has 10 windows.
2. To the right of the house with 14 steps there is a house with 2 steps.
3. 4 children live in the house with 6 windows and 14 steps.
4. The house without a child has only one neighboring house.
5. To the left of the house with 4 children there is a house with 13 windows.
6. The neighbors living to the left of the family with 2 children have no children.
7. The house with 9 windows has 10 steps.
8. The house with 2 children has 8 steps in the doorway.

2.1.3. There are 4 houses. For each house there is information about the car's color, the residents' nationality and the age of the house.

What color is the 30-year-old house?

1. In a red house there lives a Frenchman.
2. 2 houses away from the German there is a 10-year-old house.
3. The Italian lives in a black house.
4. The eldest house stands next to the 20-year-old house.
5. The Dutchman's house is 110 years old.
6. To the left of the Italian there is a gray house.
7. The white house is 20 years old.
8. 3 houses to the left of the Frenchman there is a white house.

2.1.4. There are 4 houses. For each house there is information about the residents' profession, the car brand and the age of the house.

What profession does the Volvo driver have?

1. The mechanician drives a Seat.
2. The resident of the youngest house drives a VW.
3. The 20-year-old house stands to the right of the 43-year-old house.
4. The Porsche driver's house is 43 years old.
5. The hairdresser lives next to the electrician.
6. The Seat driver's house is 16 years old.
7. The house which is to the left of the Seat driver is only 5 years old.
8. To the left of the mechanician there lives the teacher.
9. To the right of the mechanician there lives the electrician.

2.1.5. There are 4 houses. For each house there is information about the kind of plot boundary, the color and the facilities relating to cellar and loft.

What can you tell about the cellar and the loft of the house which has a wall as border?

1. 2 houses to the left of the house with cellar and without loft there is a house with a fence as plot boundary.
2. The gray house has a cellar and no loft.
3. The brown house stands between the yellow and the light blue house.
4. The yellow house has only one neighbor to the right.
5. The 2 houses without lofts stand side by side.
6. The house without cellar, but with loft stands next to a house without loft.
7. The house with hedge stands next to the house with fence.
8. One house has no cellar and no loft.
9. Only 2 houses have a cellar.
10. 2 houses have a loft.
11. The house with lattice fence is next to the house with hedge.
12. The light blue house stands between the brown and the gray house.

2.1.6. There are 4 houses. For each house there is information about the yard, the car´s color and the house´s color.

What color is the house with 2 yards?

1. One house is dark green.
2. To the right of the yellow house there is the gray house.
3. To the right of the black car there stands the red car.
4. The plot to the left of the orange house has a big yard.

5. The plot with the big yard is between two plots, of which one has no yard and the other one has a small yard.
6. In front of the gray house there stands a white car.
7. The red car stands in front of the yellow house.
8. The gray house has a big yard.
9. To the left of the gray car there stands the white car.

2.1.7. There are 4 houses. For each house there is information about the age of the house, the number of children and the number of windows.

How old is the house with 3 children?

1. To the right of the house with 5 children there stands a 8-year-old house.
2. The 50-year-old house has 15 windows.
3. The house with one child is 45 years old.
4. 2 children live in the house with 12 windows.
5. The right house is 8 years old.
6. 2 houses away from the 5 children there lives a family with only one child.
7. The 45-year-old house has 6 windows.
8. To the left of the house with 15 windows there stands a 130-year-old house.
9. Next to the house with 6 windows there stands a house with 5 windows.

2.1.8. There are 4 houses. For each house there is information about the number of steps, about the yard and about the car brand.

How many steps does the house of the Mercedes driver have?

1. The house without yard has 4 steps.
2. To the right of the house with 4 steps there stands a house with 6 steps.
3. The Peugeot stands next to the VW.
4. The house with one yard stands to the right of the house with 3 yards.
5. The Fiat stands in front of the house with 2 yards.
6. The house with 2 steps stands to the right of the house with 12 steps.
7. The Peugeot stands next to the Fiat.
8. Next to the house with 2 steps there stands a house with 4 steps.

2.1.9. There are 4 houses. For each house there is information about the pet, about the owner´s nationality and the number of children.

What kind of pet do the 2 children have?

1. The family with the dog has one child.
2. The Finn does not live next to the Italian.
3. The right neighbor of the family with 4 children has a dog.
4. 2 houses away from the family with the bird there lives a family with a cat.
5. The family with 3 children has a bird.
6. Next to the cat there lives a mouse.
7. The Italian lives to the left of the Spaniard.
8. The Spaniard has 4 children.

9. Next to the family with one child there lives a family with 3 children.
10. The Italian does not live next to the Swiss.

2.1.10. There are 4 houses. For each house there is information about the plot boundary, the age of the house and the owner's profession.

How old is the house with the walls?

1. The official's house has no border.
2. The policeman's house is 34 years old.
3. 2 houses away from the 14-year-old house there stands one with a hedge.
4. The house with fence is 14 years old.
5. To the right of the trainer there lives an official.
6. The youngest house has only one neighbor.
7. The rightmost house is 34 years old.
8. The house without border is 70 years old.
9. The hairdresser's house is 10 years old.
10. The house with hedge stands to the right of the official's one.

2.2. Level of difficulty: high

2.2.1. There are 4 houses. For each house there is information about the age and the size of the owner, the house's color and the car brand.

What kind of brand does the owner of the white house drive?

1. In a gray house there lives the 46-year-old man.
2. The Fiat driver and the Opel driver are neighbors.
3. The owner of the green house is 191 cm tall.
4. On average the owners are 41.5 years old.
5. The 42-year-old man is 191 cm tall.
6. The youngest one drives a VW.
7. The man living next to the brown house drives an Opel and is 181 cm tall.
8. In the second house to the left there lives the youngest one.
9. One owner is 40 years old.
10. The 42-year-old man's neighbor is 46 years old.
11. The 182 cm tall man lives in a brown house.
12. The VW driver is 6 cm smaller than his left neighbor.
13. The Audi driver is 188 cm tall.

2.2.2. There are 4 houses. For each house there is information about the house's age and the color, the size of the plot and the number of children.

How many children live on the 800 m² plot?

1. The gray house stands next to the red house.
2. 2 children live in the 10-year-old house.
3. To the left of the family with one child there lives a family with 4 children.

4. The 3 children live on a 1,500 m² plot.
5. The house with 4 children is 15 years old.
6. The green house stands next to the red house.
7. To the right of the 45-year-old house there stands a 31-year-old house.
8. 3 children live in the white house.
9. The right neighbor of the 2 children has a 1,200 m² plot.
10. Next to the biggest plot there lives a family with one child on a 950 m² plot.
11. One child lives in the gray house.

2.2.3. There are 4 houses. For each house there is information about the owner's age and profession, the dislikes and likes and about the car brand.

How old is the baker?

1. Next to the Opel driver there lives the BMW driver.
2. The painter's right neighbor is 8 years younger than himself.
3. The eldest person likes pizza, but no pasta.
4. The 35-year-old man dislikes pasta and pizza.
5. Left to the person who likes pasta and dislikes pizza there lives a person who dislikes pasta and pizza.
6. The 43-year-old man likes pasta and pizza.
7. The electrician drives an Opel.
8. Left to the electrician there lives somebody who likes pasta and dislikes pizza.
9. The Seat driver is a painter.
10. The businessman dislikes pizza.
11. The electrician is 24 years older than his neighbor.
12. The Volvo driver's right neighbor is 35 years old.

2.2.4. There are 4 houses. For each house there is information about the age and the size of the owner, about the number of children and about the pet.

How old is the 188 cm tall owner?

1. The bird owner's neighbor is 191 cm tall.
2. The cat owner's neighbors does not have children.
3. The owner of the house without children is 20 cm smaller than the cat owner.
4. The cat owner is 2 years younger than the neighbor who lives 2 houses away.
5. The 43-year-old man is 187 cm tall.
6. The hamster lives 3 houses to the right of the cat.
7. The fish owner is 45 years old.
8. The 49-year-old man has 2 children.
9. The 3 children have fish.
10. The neighbor of the family with one child is 51 years old.

2.2.5. There are 4 houses. For each house there is information about the property value, the number of windows and steps, the color and the age.

How many windows does the house with a value of the property of 250,000€ have?

1. The brown house is between the white and the green house.
2. One house is 50 years old.
3. The house with 5 steps stands on a plot which is 60,000€ more expensive than the plot to the right.
4. The plot of the house with 7 steps has a value of 150,000€.
5. The house with the 150,000€ plot has 4 windows less than the neighboring house.

6. 14 windows has the house with a value of the property of 120,000€.
7. 180,000€ is the value of the property on which a 20-year-old house stands.
8. The green house is next to the gray house.
9. The house with 6 windows is to the left of the house with 8 windows.
10. The house with the fewest steps is to the left of the house with the most steps.
11. The green house has 5 steps.
12. The house with 2 steps is 80 years old.
13. The gray house has 4 steps.
14. The 40-year-old house is to the left of the 20-year-old house.
15. The house standing to the right of the gray house has got one step more.

2.2.6. There are 4 houses. For each house there is information about the pet, the owner's profession and his hobbies. Besides that, the attitude toward 2 sports and 2 foods is known.

Which hobby does the agent have?

1. One person likes apples, but no plums.
2. The hockey player dislikes handball.
3. The owner who dislikes soccer and apples loves to solve riddles.
4. One person dislikes handball, but likes soccer.
5. The veterenarian owns a hamster.
6. The car lover's left neighbor likes handball and plums.
7. The fish owner dislikes handball.
8. The businessman lives in the leftmost house.
9. One person dislikes apples and plums, but likes soccer.
10. The bird owner likes soccer and handball.
11. The businessman's neighbor plays chess.
12. The bird owner lives 2 houses away from the dog owner, and likes apples and plums.
13. The mechanician's left neighbor dislikes apples and plums.
14. The owner who likes apples and dislikes plums also dislikes soccer and handball.
15. The chess player owns a dog and likes apples.

2.2.7. There are 4 houses. For each house there is information about the age and the house's color, the number of children and the car's color and brand.

What color is the car of the family with 3 children?

1. The 48-year-old man lives 2 houses to the right of the 40-year-old man.

2. An Opel stands to the left of the Renault.
3. The 60-year-old house is to the right of the 51-year-old house.
4. 2 children live in the house with the white BMW.
5. For each house, you get 100 if you add up the age of the house and the age of the owner.
6. The 57-year-old man drives a Renault.
7. The yellow car stands between the gray and the blue car.
8. In the 43-year-old house there live 3 children more than in the house to the right.
9. The family with 5 children has a blue car.
10. In the house with the Opel there lives one child less than 2 houses away.
11. The VW-driver is 49 years old.

2.2.8. There are 4 houses. For each owner there is information about the hair color, the age, the profession, the attitude toward smoking and drinking, and the owner´s opinion about the card games skat and poker.

How old is the trainer?

1. The mechanician´s neighbor has red hair.
2. The 45-year-old man is blond.
3. The hairdresser smokes, but does not drink.
4. The agent´s left neighbor has brown hair.
5. The agent likes smoking, drinking and poker, but dislikes skat.
6. The 35-year-old man dislikes smoking and drinking.
7. The neighbor of the skat- and poker fan dislikes skat and poker.
8. The neighbor of the black-haired-man is blond.
9. The skat-player who dislikes poker, likes drinking, but dislikes smoking.
10. The left neighbor of the youngest one is 10 years older.
11. Both smokers live farthest apart from each other.
12. The hairdresser dislikes skat and poker.
13. The 49-year-old man lives to the right of the 41-year-old man.

2.2.9. There are 4 houses. For each owner there is information about the profession, the size and the age. Besides that, there is information about the value of the property and the car brand.

What profession does the 55-year old man have?

1. The author is with a height of 190 cm exactly 1cm taller than his neighbor.

2. The most valuable plot is next to the lowest priced plot.
3. The author lives 2 houses away from the teacher.
4. The second largest person drives a Porsche.
5. The teacher's plot has a value of 210,000€.
6. The right neighbor of the Fiat driver drives a BMW.
7. The businessman is 182 cm tall.
8. The plot of the youngest one has the lowest value.
9. The driver is 41 years old.
10. The plot of the 41-year-old man has a value of 160,000€.
11. One person is 32 years old.
12. One plot is 10,000 € less expensive than the driver's plot.
13. The plot of the Seat driver has a value of 190,000€.
14. The 35-year-old man has two neighbors.
15. The youngest one lives in the left house.
16. The driver's left neighbor is 175 cm tall.

2.2.10. There are 4 houses. For each owner there is information about the monthly income, the size and the age. Besides that, there is information about the age of the house and the kind of plot boundary.

How old is the house with the walls?

1. The house with fir trees as boundary is 60 years old.
2. The owner who earns 2,100€, has a 70-year-old neighboring house to the right.
3. The 38-year-old man is 187 cm tall, and earns 2,800€.
4. The 181 cm tall owner is 7 years older than his left neighbor.
5. The owner with a fence as plot boundary earns 3,400€.
6. The left of 2 neighbors is 4 cm smaller.
7. The 29-year-old man earns the least, and has a hedge as plot boundary.
8. The right one of 2 neighbors is 9 cm smaller.
9. One person is 41 years old.
10. The neighbor of the 29-year-old man is 9 years older, and he earns 1,500€ more.
11. The house with hedge is 15 years younger than the house to the right.
12. One person is 34 years old.
13. One resident's right neighbor is 2 cm taller.
14. The house of the 190 cm tall owner is 12 years old.
15. The 185 cm tall owner has a 45-year-old house.

2.3. Level of difficulty: very high
Note: For combinations of likes and dislikes for miscellaneous things there is always just one combination possible.

2.3.1. There are 5 houses. For each owner there is information about the number of children, the hair color, the age and the attitude toward 3 different foods. Besides that, there is information about the car brand and the house's color.
What hair color does the Audi driver have?

1. The owner who dislikes pasta and potatoes, but likes rice, is 4 years older than his neighbor.
2. The house with the most children is brown.
3. The family with 2 children eats pasta, but no rice.
4. The owner with gray hair lives in a yellow house.
5. The Opel driver's left neighbor has red hair.
6. One house is gray.
7. The 63-year-old man dislikes pasta and rice.
8. The brown-haired man's left neighbor drives a Renault.
9. The left neighbor has 2 children less.
10. In the house with 6 children, no pasta but rice is eaten.
11. Nobody likes potatoes in the brown house nor in the house next to it.
12. The right one of 2 neighbors has 4 children more.
13. The family with 4 children eats rice and potatoes, but no pasta.
14. The right resident of 2 neighbors has one child less.
15. 2 houses away from the 40-year-old man there lives a black-haired man.
16. The neighbor of the 51-year-old man is 12 years older.
17. The family who only likes pasta has a white house.
18. The VW driver is blond.
19. The BMW driver has 3 children, and likes potatoes.
20. The black-haired man dislikes potatoes.
21. The family with one child eats rice and pasta.
22. One person is 44 years old.
23. The right neighbor has 3 children less.
24. The 34-year-old man is blond, and lives in a green house.

2.3.2. There are 5 houses. For each owner there is information about the name, the age, the profession, the income, the car's color and the attitude toward different sports.

Who owns the yellow car?

1. The person with the highest income lives in the leftmost house.
2. Steffen likes swimming, cycling and jogging.
3. The agent is 21 years older than his neighbor, and he earns 3,600€.
4. The woman's right neighbor earns 350€ more.
5. A brown car stands in front of the house next to the female caregiver's house.
6. One person has a neighbor to the left who earns 400€ more.
7. Beate has the highest income of them all.
8. The woman who dislikes cycling and jogging, but likes swimming, drives a black car.
9. The right one of 2 female neighbors earns 700€ less.
10. The 42-year-old woman likes cycling and dislikes jogging.
11. Beate is 43 years old, dislikes jogging and works as a saleslady.
12. Susi's neighbor likes jogging, and dislikes cycling.
13. As a craftsman, Maik earns 2,850€.
14. The female attorney earns 2,500€.
15. In total, 2 of 5 people dislike swimming.
16. The person who dislikes swimming drives a gray car.
17. The 29-year-old man's neighbor is 13 years older.
18. Susi's neighbor earns 3,200€.
19. The man who only likes jogging drives a green car.
20. The two people with the highest income like swimming and cycling.
21. Steffen's neighbor Marika likes cycling, and dislikes jogging.

22. The 51-year-old man´s female neighbor likes to go swimming.
23. The left one of two neighboring people earns 500€ more.
24. The female cargiver is 30 years old.

2.3.3. There are 5 houses. For each owner there is information about the hobby, the profession and the hair color. Besides that, there is information about the car brand and color. The house's color is known too.

What car stands in front of the white house?

1. The stamp collector lives in the green house.
2. A cardplayer lives to the left of the agent.
3. The owner of the black car has only one neighbor.
4. The orange house is between two houses.
5. The owner of the white car dislikes climbing and motorcycles.
6. A gray Mercedes stands to the right of the businessman's house.
7. The climber has a brown house.
8. A man with bald head lives next to the mechanician.
9. Neither a Fiat nor a Mercedes stands next to the Opel.
10. The red-haired man has a gray house.
11. The trader lives 2 houses away from the businessman, and dislikes riddles and stamps.
12. The brown-haired man lives next to the black-haired man.
13. Neither a VW nor a Mercedes stands next to the BMW.
14. Neither a black nor a white car stands next to the brown car.
15. The businessman's right neighbor likes motorcycles.
16. The blond trainer likes riddles.
17. The climber lives next to the gray house.
18. The VW owner has only one neighbor.
19. The Mercedes driver has only one neighbor.
20. Neither a VW nor a Opel stands next to the Fiat.
21. The businessman drives a Fiat.

2.3.4. There are 6 houses. For each owner, the profession, the age, the favorite dish and the favorite drink are known. Besides that, there is information about the house's color and the car brand.

What profession does the Opel driver have?

1. The coffee drinker's right neighbor likes to drink tea.
2. The water drinker's neighbor likes cocoa.
3. The coffee drinker likes bockwurst.
4. The 45-year-old teacher likes spaghetti.
5. The green house stands between the brown and the red house.
6. The baker's neighbor is 6 years younger.
7. The Fiat stands between the Porsche and the Peugeot.
8. The tea drinker's neighbor likes salad.
9. The 31-year-old man likes to eat steak.
10. The 26-year-old man likes to eat hamburger.
11. A glazier lives 2 houses away from the agent.
12. The saleslady is 34 years old.
13. The salad eater's right neighbor is 24 years younger.
14. The white house stands to the right of the orange house.
15. The owner of the yellow house likes juice.
16. The Porsche stands in front of the house which stands to the left of the white house.
17. The Audi driver's neighbor is 50 years old.
18. The agent likes to eat steak.
19. One person likes milk and potato salad.
20. The 51-year-old man is a baker.
21. The butcher drives a VW.
22. The coffee drinker's neighbor is 17 years older.
23. The glazier's house is red.
24. The Audi driver likes hamburger.

2.3.5. There are 5 houses. For each owner the name, the size, the age and the attitude toward miscellaneous foods, as well as the attitude respective several leisure activities is known. Besides that, the houses' ages are known as well.

Who lives in the 50-year-old house?

1. The person who only likes hiking, does not eat fruit, and lives in a 43-year-old house.
2. The 51-year-old Kerstin likes pizza, salad and fruit.
3. 2 women love to go shopping.
4. 2 people like flying.
5. Hans is 6 years older than his female neighbor.
6. The 171cm tall woman is 51 years old.
7. The tallest woman is 8 cm taller than the smallest woman.
8. Next to the man who likes pizza there lives a woman who eats pizza and fruit.
9. Martin lives in a 70-year-old house.
10. The person who eats pizza and fruit, but no salad, likes to go hiking, loves flying, but hates to go shopping.
11. The left one of two female neighbors is 3 years younger.
12. One of the men only likes fruit, but no salad and no pizza, and the other one likes pizza and salad instead, but no fruit.
13. The 46-year-old man lives next to the 43-year-old man.
14. Next to the 189 cm tall man there lives a 165 cm tall woman.
15. Sophia dislikes flying, but loves hiking.
16. The person who dislikes pizza and fruit, but likes salad, lives in a 42-year-old house.
17. The 181 cm tall man dislikes to go shopping, hiking and flying.
18. The right one of 2 female neighbors is 8 years younger.
19. The neighbor of the 46-year-old woman dislikes to go shopping and flying.
20. The tallest one is with his 52 years not the eldest one.

21. Steffi is 165 cm tall.
22. The eldest one has a female neighbor who is 14 years younger.
23. The house in which the woman lives, who dislikes hiking, is 15 years old.
24. The eldest one´s house is the leftmost.

2.3.6. There are 5 houses. For each owner, the name, the profession, the hobby and the attitude toward miscellaneous sports and foods are known. Besides that, there is information about the cars' colors.

What hobby does the female attorney have?

1. The female kindergarden teacher goes skiing, likes handball, and dislikes hockey and volleyball.
2. The person with the yellow car likes cycling.
3. The men like to eat fish and bread.
4. The person who dislikes handball, hockey and volleyball, lives next to Tina.
5. The person who dislikes hockey, handball and volleyball, likes to listen to music.
6. The policewoman drives a red car.
7. One man likes beef and dislikes rice.
8. The person with the green car likes handball.
9. The electrician dislikes hockey, rice and beef.
10. The woman living next to the owner of the black car likes to go jogging.
11. The woman who likes rice and fish, but does not eat beef and bread, drives a green car.
12. Tim lives to the right of Beate.
13. The woman who likes rice and fish, but dislikes beef and bread, has a neighbor who dislikes rice and beef, but only likes fish and bread.
14. The person with the red car likes hockey, volleyball, fish and bread.
15. Tim lives to the left of Rolf.
16. All women like handball.
17. The doctor lives to the right of the electrician.
18. 2 people dislike bread.
19. Beate dislikes hockey and volleyball.

20. Maria dislikes rice and beef.
21. Tina lives between Maria and Rolf.
22. The brown car stands 2 houses away from the person who likes fish and bread, but dislikes rice and beef.
23. The person who likes rice, fish, hockey and beef, dislikes volleyball.
24. The person going by bike likes handball and volleyball.

2.3.7. There are 6 houses. For each owner, the name, the income, the size, the profession, the hair color and the attitude toward several leisure activities are known.

Who earns 2,100€?

1. The craftsman likes everything except from drawing.
2. The man who likes everything except from drawing is 9 cm taller than his female neighbor.
3. Tobias does not live next to Kerstin and Markus.
4. The craftsman earns with 1,500€ exactly 1,300€ less than his neighbor.
5. Kerstin's female neighbor dislikes watching TV.
6. The red-haired person lives 2 houses away from the person with bald head.
7. Stefanie does not live next to Kerstin and Markus.
8. The tallest man with a height of 191 cm lives in the rightmost house.
9. Ulf earns 1,500€.
10. Ulf does not live next to Stefanie and Tobias.
11. A smith with bald head lives next to the brown-haired man.
12. The man who likes watching TV, computer games and drawing, but dislikes reading, is 181 cm tall.
13. The technician is 181 cm tall.
14. The person who likes everything except watching TV is 167 cm tall.
15. 2 houses away from the person who likes reading and computer games, but dislikes watching TV and drawing there lives a woman who also likes computer games, but no TV, no reading and no drawing.
16. The saleslady only dislikes computer games.
17. The fair-haired woman earns 2,300€.
18. The female principal only likes computer games and nothing else.

19. The green-haired woman's neighbor earns 1,900€.
20. Markus does not live next to Kerstin.
21. The person who earns 2,800€ likes reading and computer games, but dislikes watching TV and drawing.
22. The black-haired person lives between the people who are 167 cm tall and 172 cm tall, respectively.
23. A female teacher who likes reading, computer games and drawing lives next to the red-haired woman.
24. Martina does not live next to Stefanie, Ulf and Markus.
25. The technician's neighbor is green-haired.
26. The craftsman lives next to the female principal.
27. A 177 cm tall woman lives 2 houses away from a man.
28. The person who likes reading, watching TV and drawing, but dislikes computer games, earns 1,800€.
29. The 186 cm tall person has brown hair.

2.3.8. There are 6 houses. For each owner, the nationality and the age are known. Besides that, everybody smokes a particular brand, reads special books and likes a certain sport. The house's windows' number is known.

How old is the Swiss?

1. The poem reader's neighbor smokes f6.
2. The Spaniard's neighbor is 41 years old.
3. The Englishman's left neighbor is 16 years younger.
4. One house has 8 windows.
5. The 61-year-old Cabinet-smoker lives in a house with 14 windows.
6. Between the tennis player and the volleyball player there lives somebody who likes to read short stories.
7. The Italian lives 5 houses away from the Frenchman.
8. The f6-smoker is 50 years old.
9. The tennis player lives 2 houses away from the volleyball player.
10. The Frenchman reads nonfiction books.
11. The West-smoker lives 3 houses away from the 41-year-old man.
12. The hockey player lives next to the soccer player.
13. The Pall Mall-smoker lives in a house with 12 windows.
14. The Pall Mall-smoker's neighbor reads crime thrillers.
15. The 50-year-old man's neighbor is 3 years older.
16. A person who likes magazines and sailing lives in the house with 7 windows.
17. 2 houses to the left of the West-smoker there lives a person who likes to read nonfiction books.
18. The house with 12 windows is 3 houses away from the house with 9 windows.
19. The Spaniard likes volleyball.
20. The Marlboro-smoker's neighbor smokes Davidoff.

21. The 57-year-old man´s house has 15 windows.
22. The house of the person who reads short stories has 9 windows.
23. The house with the most windows is next to the house with the fewest windows.
24. The German lives next to the 57-year-old man.
25. One person smokes Marlboro and likes dramas.
26. The German lives 2 houses away from the Englishman.

2.3.9. There are 6 houses. For each owner, the age, the income, the size and the name are known. There is also information about the house's color and the car brand.

How much does the man in the brown house earn?

1. The 43-year-old man is 181 cm tall.
2. Wolfgang's neighbor has a red house.
3. Maik drives Renault, and he is 7 cm smaller than the man who lives 3 houses away.
4. Michael lives in the rightmost house, and is 25 years younger than his neighbor.
5. The 188 cm tall man is 66 years old.
6. Maik lives 2 houses away from the Opel driver.
7. Eberhard drives a Fiat, and is 188 cm tall.
8. An Opel driver lives 2 houses away from Michael.
9. The orange house's resident is 10 years older than the person who lives 3 houses away.
10. The 51-year-old man lives between the yellow and the white house.
11. The 43-year-old man earns 2,700€.
12. The orange house is to the right of the Renault driver.
13. Bernd lives to the left of Maik, and is 56 years old.
14. The owner of the BMW earns 2,000€, lives to the right of the Renault's owner, and is 177 cm tall.
15. The Opel driver is 5 cm taller than his right neighbor.
16. The VW driver is 41 years old, and earns 1,800€.

2.3.10. There are 6 houses. For each owner, the nationality, the hobby, the profession, the learned occupation, the favorite food and the pet are known.

Which country does the „French fries eater" come from?
1. The technician has a rat, and likes chocolate.
2. The Dane lives between the Finn and the Swiss.
3. The carpenter likes soccer.
4. The agent lives between the mechanician and the brick layer.
5. The roofer lives 3 houses away from the hamster's owner, and to the left of the mechanician.
6. The brick layer with his hamster lives 2 houses away from the bird's owner.
7. The skilled salesclerk´s neighbor likes fish.
8. The dog lives between the cat and the bird.
9. The skilled clerk´s neighbor likes to go skiing.
10. One person likes handball and rice.
11. The Hungarian lives between the Swiss and the Spaniard.
12. The carpenter is a skilled clerk.
13. One person likes flying and ice cream.
14. The skilled driver´s right neighbor likes flying.
15. The person who likes pasta also likes rock climbing.
16. The Swede lives to the left of the Finn.
17. The agent is a skilled driver.
18. The skilled electrician likes chocolate.

3. Sequences of numbers

A series of numbers is given for these tasks. There is always a system behind these sequences of numbers. You have to find out these system and continue the sequence of numbers. The higher the difficulty, the more complex and ample the possible solutions. If you use the solution part to check your answers or to get a hint, please, assure that you do not see the following sequences of numbers. You should cover these with a sheet of paper.
The solution numbers are always whole numbers.

3.1. Level of difficulty: low

3.1.1.
 4 7 5 8 6 ___ ___ ___

3.1.2.
 -5 -13 -17 -15 -23 ___ ___ ___

3.1.3.
 15 21 20 17 23 ___ ___ ___

3.1.4.
 5 23 27 28 46 ___ ___ ___

3.1.5.
 -45 -41 -49 -52 -48 ___ ___ ___

3.1.6.
 10 14 9 13 7 11 6 ___ ___ ___

3.1.7.
 40 38 19 17 -2 ___ ___ ___

3.1.8.
8 6 4 8 6 ___ ___ ___

3.1.9.
14 7 3 -4 -3 -10 -14 ___ ___ ___

3.1.10.
5 1 4 0 ___ ___ ___

3.1.11.
11 22 33 30 41 ___ ___ ___

3.1.12.
31 35 41 46 50 ___ ___ ___

3.1.13.
7 12 9 7 6 11 ___ ___ ___

3.1.14.
15 10 5 0 1 -4 ___ ___ ___

3.1.15.
113 105 108 110 102 ___ ___ ___

3.1.16.
-55 -70 -80 -85 -100 ___ ___ ___

3.1.17.
-14 -10 -9 -12 -14 -10 ___ ___ ___

3.1.18.
13 25 36 46 55 ___ ___ ___

3.1.19.
0 5 -1 2 -4 1 ___ ___ ___

3.1.20.
9 3 0 3 -3 ___ ___ ___

3.2. Level of difficulty: middle

3.2.1.
4 24 8 26 6 36 12 ___ ___ ___

3.2.2.
15 3 30 35 7 70 ___ ___ ___

3.2.3.
14 42 -84 252 504 1512 ___ ___ ___

3.2.4.
3 -3 -6 2 -3 -9 ___ ___ ___

3.2.5.
2 10 9 45 47 235 234 ___ ___ ___

3.2.6.
7 3 -6 0 -4 8 0 ___ ___ ___

3.2.7.
2 -8 -4 -10 -20 -10 ___ ___ ___

3.2.8.
0 -4 -9 -1 5 1 ___ ___ ___

3.2.9.
3 -3 2 -5 6 -6 ___ ___ ___

3.2.10.
16 4 -3 1 4 1 ___ ___ ___

3.2.11.
10 5 15 -2 -1 -3 ___ ___ ___

3.2.12.
13 6 -24 -6 1 -6 24 ___ ___ ___

3.2.13.
3 -9 -18 -12 36 72 ___ ___ ___

3.2.14.
-3 -15 -5 -8 2 -10 ___ ___ ___

3.2.15.
13 0 5 0 -2 0 ___ ___ ___

3.2.16.
4 12 24 6 18 ___ ___ ___

3.2.17.
-13 -26 -22 3 6 10 35 ___ ___ ___

3.2.18.
-17 34 4 -3 6 ___ ___ ___

3.2.19.
7 -7 -14 14 28 ___ ___ ___

3.2.20.
30 6 -2 8 -16 ___ ___ ___

3.3. Level of difficulty: high

3.3.1.
4 6 3 8 1 12 ___ ___ ___

3.3.2.
-6 -5 -10 -7 -28 ___ ___ ___

3.3.3.
4 12 7 21 29 24 72 ___ ___ ___

3.3.4.
-20 -21 -19 -16 -11 -4 -13 ___ ___ ___

3.3.5.
-10 -8 -4 -9 -3 5 ___ ___ ___

3.3.6.
17 19 23 29 31 37 ___ ___ ___

3.3.7.
1 3 -1 -3 3 -5 -15 ___ ___ ___

3.3.8.
3 6 3 -2 -8 -14 -24 -48 ___ ___ ___

3.3.9.
3 12 6 18 13 52 ___ ___ ___

3.3.10.
41 42 45 43 39 38 35 37 41 42 ___ ___ ___

3.3.11.
3 4 8 11 44 49 ___ ___ ___

3.3.12.
5 8 14 23 35 ___ ___ ___

3.3.13.
-31 -29 -26 -31 -24 -13 -26 -9 ___ ___ ___

3.3.14.
-7 -4 1 4 -1 -4 -9 -6 ___ ___ ___

3.3.15.
-2 -4 -8 -5 -10 -20 -17 ___ ___ ___

3.3.16.
5 7 11 5 -3 7 ___ ___ ___

3.3.17.
5 1 5 -1 -7 -15 -135 ___ ___ ___

3.3.18.
4 2 -1 -6 -13 -24 ___ ___ ___

3.3.19.
-3 6 -18 -23 46 -138 ___ ___ ___

3.3.20.
-35 -36 -34 -31 -26 -19 -28 -17 ___ ___ ___

3.4. Level of difficulty: very high

Show patience and concentration. Partially, the pattern in the sequences of numbers are hardly apparent and can sometimes only be found by thinking outside the box.

3.4.1.
1 2 5 11 21 ___ ___ ___

3.4.2.
11 22 88 1408 18304 ___

3.4.3.
-45 -44 -41 -39 -35 -32 -27 ___ ___ ___ ___

3.4.4.
2 3 5 7 2 4 8 ___ ___ ___

3.4.5.
4 0 -6 -16 -30 ___ ___ ___

3.4.6.
15 12 8 14 10 11 13 8 14 ___ ___ ___

3.4.7.
4 6 3 9 14 7 49 60 47 2209 ___ ___ ___

3.4.8.
2 -6 -2 0 0 4 8 -24 -20 -18 54 58 71 ___ ___ ___

3.4.9.
0 1 -1 2 -4 1 -9 -2 -16 ___ ___ ___

3.4.10.
1 4 10 6 5 17 41 37 36 ___ ___ ___

3.4.11.
10 -1 -14 1 -16 -35 ___ ___ ___

3.4.12.
-3 -24 -20 -39 -33 -50 -42 ___ ___ ___ ___

3.4.13.
-8 -4 -1 -3 -2 ___ ___ ___ ___

3.4.14.
13 6 10 9 8 ___

3.4.15.
-2 1 -1 -2 -5 -1 -7 -4 ___ ___ ___ ___ ___

3.4.16.
0 2 5 15 5 10 17 51 41 ___ ___ ___ ___ ___

3.4.17.
3 7 22 111 ___ ___

3.4.18.
17 15 8 20 18 2 23 21 -4 ___ ___ ___

3.4.19.
-4 -8 -24 -20 -15 -90 -630 -622 -613 _____ _____ _____ _____

3.4.20.
2 8 24 12 14 56 168 84 88 ___ ___ ___ ___

4. Complete the formulae

Formulae are written in horizontal and vertical direction. These have gaps. It is your task to fill out the gaps so that the results are correct. Signs and numbers can be missing. The rule, „multiplication and division first, then addition and subtraction" is **not** applied. Only calculate with whole numbers. No number, not even a intermediate result, is less than zero.

4.2. Level of difficulty: low

4.1.1.

	x		=	12
x		+		
	-		=	1
=		=		
24		8		

4.1.2.

	-		=	6
+		x		
	x		=	15
=		=		
17		40		

4.1.3.

21		3	=	7
	x		=	40
=		=		
13		8		

4.1.4.

		3		=		27
	+		-			
8				=		16
=		=				
17		1				

4.1.5.

6				=		12
		+				
		7		=		12
=		=				
11						

4.1.6.

	x			=		20
+						
3		1		=		2
=		=				
8		4				

4.1.7.

16				=		4
-		x				
	+			=		14
=		=				
5		12				

4.1.8.

	+		=	13
x				
5		2	=	3
=		=		
15		5		

4.1.9.

	/	4	=	3
6	+		=	11
=		=		
6		20		

4.1.10.

9		3	=	3
		6	=	10
=		=		
5		18		

4.1.11.

14			=	4
		+		
		6	=	12
=		=		
7		16		

4.1.12.

6			=	17
		x		
	-	2	=	3
=		=		
30		22		

4.1.13.

6		6	=	12
	-		=	10
=		=		
18		12		

4.1.14.

	+	3	=	11
4			=	11
=		=		
4		21		

4.1.15.

5			=	20
x		-		
	+		=	9
=		=		
10		8		

4.1.16.

7			=	13
		x		
	-		=	1
=		=		
13		30		

4.1.17.

	/		=	1
/				
2	x		=	14
=		=		
4		15		

4.1.18.

			=	14
x				
7		6	=	1
=		=		
7		7		

4.1.19.

		9	=	4
		/		
1			=	4
=		=		
13		3		

4.1.20.

			2		=		8
	/						
4					=		8
=			=				
4			8				

4.3. Level of difficulty: middle

4.2.1.

6	/	3			=	20
				-		
3	+	7	-	3	=	7
				/		
2			/		=	2
=		=		=		
20		13		3		

4.2.2.

9			/	4	=	3
/				+		
	+	8			=	22
		/		-		
		2		5	=	9
=		=		=		
10		12		1		

79

4.2.3.

15		5		6	=	18
/				x		
3			/	2	=	5
	+	4			=	18
=		=		=		
25		3		10		

4.2.4.

20				5	=	10
/		x				
		3	+	6	=	13
				-		
	x	6			=	2
=		=		=		
8		5		2		

4.2.5.

19			/	3	=	7
		x				
4	x				=	10
5			/	3	=	4
=		=		=		
3		1		3		

4.2.6.

			-	21	=	14
		+				
6	/		+	7	=	10
-		/				
7	+		+	5	=	15
=		=		=		
23		3		15		

4.2.7.

7	+	5			=	24
		+				
			-	10	=	2
x		/				
6	/		+	8	=	11
=		=		=		
18		4		4		

4.2.8.

11			/	7	=	3
				x		
		16	-	8	=	12
/						
5	+	16			=	1
=		=		=		
3		42		36		

4.2.9.

		2	/		=	11
		+		x		
11	+			4	=	4
/				-		
2		7			=	21
=		=		=		
10		14		5		

4.2.10.

20	+	15			=	5
-		-				
14			/	6	=	7
		-				
	x		-	10	=	5
=		=		=		
9		7		3		

4.2.11.

18	+		/		=	5
x		+		+		
	+	13		7	=	22
		/				
	x			12	=	33
=		=		=		
4		5		25		

4.2.12.

15	+		/		=	5
		-				
3		8		16	=	8
/				/		
		6	-	11	=	19
=		=		=		
9		42		2		

4.2.13.

17		3		3	=	23
				x		
			x	9	=	18
x		-				
4		7			=	33
=		=		=		
28		4		30		

4.2.14.

30	/	5			=	19
				+		
20			x	2	=	32
		6	/	7	=	3
=		=		=		
25		14		8		

4.2.15.

9				31	=	53
x				-		
6	+	5			=	7
		/				
		3		9	=	14
=		=		=		
39		6		3		

4.2.16.

14	x	3				=	27
		+					
	/		+	7		=	15
/		/					
23			/	8		=	2
=		=		=			
2		1		16			

4.2.17.

56		2			=	4
		+				
8		9		4	=	13
		x		x		
	-		+	7	=	17
=		=		=		
20		33		21		

4.2.18.

			/	5	=	2
+				x		
		11	x	3	=	60
8	x	4			=	39
=		=		=		
3		4		8		

4.2.19.

		8	/	5	=	5
		/				
	+	4			=	18
/		x				
3	+	13			=	13
=		=		=		
8		26		36		

4.2.20.

32			x	7	=	14
		/				
		10	x	1	=	12
5		8		4	=	10
=		=		=		
21		11		2		

4.4. Level of difficulty: high

4.3.1.

12		14	/	2		10	=	3
		/		+				
3	x		+	5		5	=	16
-		+		-		+		
10	+	8		6	x		=	21
						/		
2			+		/	3	=	3
=		=		=		=		
13		20		2		4		

4.3.2.

44	-	34		3		5	=	6
		/		+				
	+			5	/	9	=	2
+		-		/		-		
	+	3	-		x	3	=	18
x		/		+				
2		7	/		+	8	=	11
=		=		=		=		
22		2		5		19		

4.3.3.

	x	3		30	/	8	=	3
/						/		
	+	5	/	7	+	4	=	6
		x		-				
7		4	-	15	+	7	=	20
x		-		/				
3	x		/	2		6	=	21
=		=		=		=		
27		22		4		20		

4.3.4.

32	-	12		2		8	=	5
/		/		+				
	/	4	x		+	9	=	25
+		+		+				
6	+		/	5	x		=	21
		x				/		
5	-	3		3	x		=	24
=		=		=		=		
2		36		5		6		

4.3.5.

14	-		x	3		3	=	36
/				+		+		
	+		/	5		4	=	6
x		/		/				
8	-	6	+		+		=	13
		+		+		+		
10	+	7		9		9	=	17
=		=		=		=		
6		12		10		30		

4.3.6.

34	+		/	7		3	=	2
/		x		+		+		
17	-		/	5	+		=	14
		/		+		+		
	x	4			x		=	24
/		+		/		-		
3			+	8	/	2	=	8
=		=		=		=		
3		9		4		15		

4.3.7.

12	/	6	x	15			=	22
+		+		+		+		
7	+		/	5			=	7
		/		/		+		
	x	3	-		x	3	=	24
/		-		x		/		
5			+		/	2	=	8
=		=		=		=		
3		1		30		8		

4.3.8.

40		10	x	3		3	=	15
/		+		/		+		
8	/	4	+	1	+	10	=	13
		/		x		+		
	+	7	x		-		=	33
				+				
5			x	2			=	13
=		=		=		=		
10		11		17		2		

4.3.9.

19	+	6	/	5			=	2
x		+				+		
		4	-		x	3	=	3
		+		+		+		
	/	3	+		/	5	=	2
/				/				
10	x		-	2			=	4
=		=		=		=		
3		16		6		4		

4.3.10.

13	+	12	/			1	=	4
-		/				+		
10			x		-	5	=	13
x				+		x		
			x	7	+	5	=	19
		/		/				
	+	2			+		=	28
=		=		=		=		
19		3		3		13		

4.3.11.

13			x	3	-		=	26
-		+						
		8	+		+	5	=	23
/		+		+		x		
	+	13	/	5		5	=	8
				/		-		
9	+				+	7	=	10
=		=		=		=		
27		2		2		38		

4.3.12.

				/	3	-	4	=	3
-				+					
8	+	8		6	+			=	19
		x		/		+			
		9	-	3		5		=	17
/		-				-			
4	+				/	8		=	3
=		=		=		=			
4		21		8		10			

4.3.13.

39	/		+	11				=	2
-						/			
		11	-		+	6		=	28
/		-		+					
2	+	9		3				=	1
		x		/		-			
			/	4	x	6		=	12
=		=		=		=			
14		25		5		20			

4.3.14.

		7	-		x	12	=	36
+		+				+		
11	-		+			6	=	19
/				/		/		
		8	+	3	/		=	13
+		+		+				
7			+	10	/	7	=	3
=		=		=		=		
11		6		15		63		

4.3.15.

				-	4	+	18	=	19
-					x		/		
20	-					x	6	=	18
+		-							
10	+	1			5	/		=	4
		/			+		x		
	-	3	+		6			=	9
=		=			=		=		
2		6			23		14		

4.3.16.

				-	5	-	13	=	8
					+		+		
7			/		6	+	7	=	10
/		-			-				
		12	/		8	+		=	9
x		+					/		
5	+	14	+			-		=	15
=		=			=		=		
25		15			8		3		

4.3.17.

		19	+		/	5	=	4
/		-				x		
4	+	4			-	6	=	29
				-				
			-	7	+		=	11
/		+			-	/		
7	+	3			+	5	=	6
=		=		=		=		
2		26		13		5		

4.3.18.

			/	14	x	9	=	18
						+		
35	/				-	3	=	16
/		+		/		-		
3	+	7	/			8	=	13
-		/		-				
		7	+	4	/		=	5
=		=		=		=		
13		2		9		7		

4.3.19.

4		3		15			=	9
+		-		/				
		1	/	3	+	17	=	20
				+		/		
	-				/	5	=	2
+		/				-		
38	/	2	-				=	20
=		=		=		=		
39		5		7		1		

4.3.20.

				5		2	=	4
/						x		
13			-		/	6	=	3
x		x		+		+		
4	+	7			-		=	7
		-		+				
		13	x	3		1	=	53
=		=		=		=		
7		36		10		19		

5. Textriddles

5.2. The relocation

Martin and Steffi move in together in a new apartment. Some friends help them on the day of the relocation. The relocation starts at 9 am. All of them take off their jackets and valuables in the apartment. Afterward, they start working. They have lunch around noon. Martin would like to order pizza for everybody. Reaching for his jacket, he recognizes that his wallet is missing. His watch which he took off for the manual labor is missing, too. The same happens to Steffi. Shocked, the other helpers check for their valuables, too. All people who have deposited their properties in the apartment got robbed. Maik and Thomas are the only ones who did not put their properties in the apartment. Nothing has been stolen from them. Soon, both are suspected. But was it really one of those two? Martin assumes responsibility and investigates. He knows that it took the thief at least a quarter of an hour to search through all items which were spread in the apartment. The simple question is: Who was alone in the apartment and had enough time to steal all the valuables?
Tobias, Steffen and Martina arrived on schedule at 9 am. They went into the apartment and had a cup of coffee. Then Martin and Steffi went with Martina and Steffen in the cellar to show them something. It was around 9:15 am, when the four left the apartment. Tom, Kerstin, Markus and Bernd arrived at 9:45 am. When they came into the staircase, they immediatly met Martin and Steffen. First, the four located the new apartment. When they went into the apartment, Tobias stood smoking on the balcony and wanted to get started, finally. Tom, Kerstin, Markus and Bernd took off their jackets and valuables, and were ready to start. At that time it was 10:15 am. Maik and Thomas were waiting downstairs at the transporter.

Steffi stayed with Tobias, Martina and Kerstin in the apartment. Martin and the others got the first loading. After a short coordination, Markus and Bernd carried up the first piece of furniture at 10:30 am. Afterward, the helpers carried up one piece of furniture after the other into the apartment. It went so well that the first loading was finished at 11:15 am. Meanwhile, Martina and Steffi were working in the cellar and were back again in the apartment at 11 am. Then, Martina and Kerstin went down to the transporter and were talking, while the others were carring up the furniture. Tobias helped Martin and Maik with the last piece of furniture, because it was pretty bulky. It took a quarter of an hour until they arrived at the apartment.

Short after 11:15 am, the second transporter arrived. Martin's father drove this one. But he had bad backache for some time for which reason he was just waiting until all was unloaded. Martin, Maik, Thomas, Tobias and Steffen carried up the second loading. The others worked in the apartment. Tobias and Steffen carried some things into the cellar. At that time it was 11:30 am. They met Steffi, Martina and Tom in the cellar. They assembled a closet there. Maik and Thomas brought the rest into the apartment. About 11:45 am, Martin asked Bernd for assistance to carry the last pieces. Tobias, Steffen and Maik have withdrawn themselves a bit. Steffi was a little bit upset about that and stood with Martina and Kerstin in the staircase. Markus, Tom and Thomas were in the apartment and assembled a wall closet. At least, they started with it, because it was already 11:45 am. By and by, all arrived for lunch in the apartment.

5.3. Time zones

Five friends would like to make a trip around the world. All of them start the same day in Germany. The individual arrival time is already integrated into the time spent at the respective traveling destination and is therefore not listed separately.

Beate travels 2 time zones eastbound. She stays there for 2 days. Susan and Rolf travel even 6 time zones westward. Susan stays there for 4 days and Rolf stays 1 day longer. On the 5th day, Susan flies, just like Bernd does, 3 time zones eastbound. Both stay at their place for 3 days. Tim travels even 10 time zones eastbound and stays there for 10 days. On her 3rd day, Beate travels 8 time zones westward and stays there for 8 days. On his 8th day, Bernd travels 2 time zones eastbound, where he meets Susan at the airport, coincidentally. Both stay there for 4 days. Rolf travels one time zone eastbound on his 6th and 7th day. On his 8th day, he covers exactly the same number of time zones heading east, as Susan does on her 8th day. There he spends 11 days. Beate, however, prefers to travel westward on her 11th day. She travels 10 time zones and spends 12 days. Tim meets Beate at the airport on his 11th day. He only spends 3 days before traveling 5 time zones westward. There he spends 7 days. Susan travels another 8 time zones eastbound on her 12th day. There she spends the last 10 days of her vacation.

Question: Tim would like to call Susan on his last day of vacation. What time does he have to call in order to reach Susan at 7 pm?

5.4. Murder among colleagues

Wolfgang Schmidt has founded a new company. He employs 8 people in all. In order that they all get to know each other, he invites the young team into a hut deep in the woods. That way, he aims to form a successful team. The team, including Wolfgang Schmidt, meets at the hut on a Saturday morning. It is about 10 am, when Mr. Schmidt officially welcomes all. During brunch time until noon, they start to get to know each other. Around noon, Wolfgang Schmidt points out the possible activities nearby to all visitors. In that way, he hopes that an intensive contact developes.
All spend their time on activities. Mr. Schmidt seems to be disappeared, because nobody has seen him for the whole day. In the evening, it is about 10:30 pm, a female colleague searches for him. Finally, she finds Wolfgang Schmidt murdered in his room.
The colleague, Ms. Maria Schulz, calls the police immediatly. The following facts are clear for the investigators:
1. The perpetrator has to be one of the team. He had access to the house and was well versed in it. Also a stranger would have attracted attention in this remote area.
2. Because the people do not know each other, the offender must have acted alone. The investigators exclude that more criminals worked together in this short time.
3. The time of the crime is between 3 pm and 8 pm.
4. The death occurred quickly. The offender has slightly edited the crime scene to cover up his tracks. The corpse has not been moved after death. The entire act must have taken about 15 minutes.

Who murdered Wolfgang Schmidt?

The police interrogate all individuals.

Maria Schulz says,
"I played a board game with Ms. Thomson and two other people after noon. Then, it was about 4 pm, I talked with Martin. It was a pleasant conversation and took a while. We went for a walk while we were talking. We came back into the house about 5 pm and went to the sitting area. Klaus Stein joined us shortly after. Ms. Thomson also came to us around 5:45 pm. I went to the barn around 6:30 pm. It is right behind the house. I met Martina Fränkel there. We stayed in the barn till dinner at about 8:15 pm."

Martina Fränkel says,
"I went with Mr. Stein and Mr. Wegener to the lake at about 3 pm. There is the boathouse. If you hurry, it takes about 15 minutes to go. Mr. Wegener left us a little earlier, because he would like to meet Maria Schulz in the house. That is, what they planned to do. Meanwhile, Steffen Reif came to the lake. The three of us went back to the house at 4 pm. We got lost in the house and ended up in Mr. Schmidt's room. It was between 4:15 pm and 4:30 pm. After that, it must have been 5:15 pm, Mr. Reif and I, we went back to the lake. He met someone at the boathouse around 6 pm. I watched them for a while and then I went to the barn, where I had an appointment with Ms. Schulz at 6:30 pm. Around 6:45 pm, Mr. Wegener joined us. Steffen Reif came back to the barn at 7:45 pm. We all stayed up there till dinner."

Klaus Stein says,
"I spent a lot of time with Ms. Fränkel. At the beginning, we were at the lake together with Mr. Wegener. But he left prematurely. It was around 5:15 pm, when I left Ms. Fränkel and joined a conversation between Martin Wegener and another woman. This lasted till 6:30 pm, because afterward, I helped with the preparation of dinner. Ms. Wenk and Ms. Thomson can confirm that. Mr. Wegener had only helped for a quarter of an hour. Then

we set the table and prepared everything. We had dinner at about 8:15 pm."

Martin Wegener says,
"Initially, I was at the lake. I went back to the house at 3:45 pm, where I met Ms. Schulz. We spent a lot of time together. It was 6:30 pm, when I started to help with the preparation for dinner. But I did not like it and so I went to the barn immediately. I was not feeling very well with that. Ms. Wenk, for example, started with preparing at 6:15 pm. And I just sloped off. There were 2 other women in the barn. I do not remember who it was. I drank some beers over there, while I was waiting for dinner. Shortly after 8 pm, it was finally time for dinner."

Steffen Reif says,
"I arrived at the lake at 3:30 pm. I went with Martina and Klaus back to the house around 4 pm. We have lost our way a bit and then ended up in the room of the boss. Unfortunately, he was not there. I have not seen him all day. We talked a while and then Martina and I went back to the lake at 5:15 pm. I had an appointment with Kai Fischer at the boatshouse around 6 pm.
After I had met Mr. Fischer, I still could see Ms. Fränkel for fifteen minutes at the lake. Then she was gone. We stayed there for a long while, until I went back to the barn at 7:30 pm. Again, I met Ms. Fränkel and 2 or 3 others. Then we stayed till dinner."

Ullrike Thomson says,
"Maria Schulz, Kerstin Wenk, Kai Fischer and I, we played a palor game at about 2:30 pm. It was quite funny. We played till 4 pm. Afterward, I went to the lake and paddled by boat. Ms. Wenk and Mr. Fischer went to the lake, too. I paddled till 5:30 pm, and then I went back to the house. When I arrived, I talked for a while with Mr. Stein and Mr. Wegener. Then we prepared everything

for dinner and set the table at 6:30 pm. It took us till shortly after 8 pm.

Kerstin Wenk says,
"We played a board game till 4 pm. However, Ms. Schulz was a bit outrageous. She can't lose and left us angrily around 3:30 pm. Then Ms. Thomson, Mr. Fischer and I, we went to the lake. Ms. Thomson rowed out with the boat. Mr. Fischer and I, we walked through the nature close by. Now and then, we have watched Ms. Thomson rowing. I went back to the house shortly after 6 pm. Mr. Fischer stayed there, because he wanted to meet somebody at the boatshouse. I took care of dinner from 6:15 pm. First, the others have only watched me and later they helped me. Afterward, we set the table and could serve all guests around 8:15 pm."

Kai Fischer says,
"I spent my time with Ms. Wenk till 6 pm. First, we played for a while, and then we went to the boatshouse. Ms. Schulz has already left our round at 3:30 pm. She got annoyed, because she always lost the game. I met Steffen at the boatshouse at 6 pm. We spent the rest of the evening there till we went back to the house for dinner. This was served shortly after 8 pm."

One of the people must have been alone to commit the crime. Who did have the opportunity for that?

5.5. 4 friends

What can you surely tell about the person with 2 children?

In spite of his age, the youngest one has the most vacation. The oldest one is not the person with the least vacation. The most lightweight man of all has the least vacation. The heaviest of all is also the tallest. The smallest is the oldest one. The tallest of all is neither the youngest, nor does he have the least vacation. The most lightweight one has the most children. The smallest one has the least children. No children has the one who is neither the youngest nor the oldest one.

5.6. Who stole the motorcycle?

Tom gives a party for his friends. His house is spacious and has a big yard as well. Guests are Thomas, Martin, David, Alex,
Tobias, Ulf, Bernd, Maik and Johann. Johann comes with his new motorcycle. The first guests arrive at Tom´s house at 8 pm.
It is 4:30 am, when Johann´s girlfriend calls. Johann´s motorcycle was found. It has bad scratches and lies in the ditch. The patrolman found the motorcycle around 4 am.
If you hurry, it takes three quarters of an hour from the accident scene to Tom´s house by foot. The offender must be one of the friends, because the key has been taken out of Johann´s jacket.
It is clear that at least one hour is necessary to cause the accident and get back to the party. The following statements can be made about the evening:

Bernd says,
"Ulf, Tobias and I, we were at Tom´s house at 9:30 pm and first, we ate. On our way to Tom´s house, we met David. Then, he also sat at the dining table. We surely have been eating for an hour."

Martin says,
"David, Thomas and I, we arrived at 8 pm. Then, David went right back outside. He felt sick from the ride. But Thomas can testify that we have been drinking beer for about 2 hours. I felt very sick, too. Somehow, I don't know anything else after that."

Tom says,
"I still worked in the kitchen at 8 pm. Johann arrived at the party around 9 pm and helped in the kitchen. We were done at 10:30 pm.

Maik says,
"I arrived with Alex around 9:30 pm. I wanted to play drinking games. First, I played alone. Alex felt sorry about that and started to play with me. Later, at 10:30 pm, even Bernd, Ulf and Tobias joined us. I think it was around 11:00 pm, when David showed us a really good game that we played until midnight."

Alex says,
"I played with Maik on the console. We played for quite a long time. I think from 0:30 am to 2:30 am. Thomas joined us around 1:30 am.

Tom says,
"We played poker. First, I only played with David. It was around 11:30 pm. After about half an hour, Bernd, Tobias and Ulf joined us, too. In total, we surely played until 1:30 am.

Johann says,
"Thomas and I, we went for a walk around 10:30 pm. After about one hour, we came back and I already realized that the key was gone. We searched for it for an eternity. We did not give up until

about 1:00 am. I thought, that it would pop up again sooner or later."

Tobias says,
"Johann and I, we played on the console once again around 3 am. Maik joined us at 3:30 am. Then, we played until the call."

Tom says,
"I found Martin in the toilet around 11:00 pm. He has certainly slept there for a while. He was completely drunk. Then, I put him to bed. He slept there for the rest of the evening. I am quite sure about that."

David says,
"I was with Johann and Tobias in the yard. That was around 1:30 am. We stayed there for one hour. At about 2 am, Tom, Ulf and Bernd joined us. They stayed outside for a while."

Alex says,
"Later on, David, Thomas and I, we went in the yard once again. It was about 3 am. There we met Tom, Bernd and Ulf. We all stayed outside until about 4 am."

Who stole the motorcycle, piled it and came back to the party afterward?

5.7. 5 people

In the following text 5 people are described. The description only refers to specific things that they do not like.

Task: One person dislikes more things than each other person does. What are the things?

Exactly 2 people dislike alcohol. However, even 3 people are averse to smoking. One person likes neither alcohol nor smoking. 2 people dislike car racing. One of this people dislikes alcohol and the other person dislikes smoking. 2 people dislike soccer. One person only likes sport, but no soccer. The other person who dislikes soccer also dislikes smoking. Apart from that, the person likes everything. One person dislikes car racing, but smokes. This person also dislikes candy.

5.8. 6 colleagues – what they like and dislike

6 colleagues have their own opinion about certain food. They like or dislike it. If no statement is made, nothing is known about it. In that case, the persons have no reference to this food.

Answer the following question:
One person dislikes more things than each other person does. What things does the person dislike?

There are 2 colleagues who like coffee. But they do not drink wine. Of the two colleagues who drink wine, one likes spaghetti, but the other dislikes it. Only 2 colleagues like spaghetti. One colleague dislikes spaghetti. 2 colleagues who dislike pork, bear no reference to coffee and spaghetti. The one person who dislikes spaghetti likes pork. One colleague who likes coffee, bears no reference to spaghetti. Of the two colleagues who like spaghetti, one likes coffee, but the other dislikes it. The colleague who likes coffee and spaghetti, does not eat fish. However, all colleagues like fish who dislike pork. All people who do not eat pork, also do not eat curd. Only that one who does not eat fish, eats curd. 4 colleagues like pineapple. Among other things, that colleague likes pineapple who likes spaghetti, but does not drink coffee. Of the two colleagues who dislike pineapple, one likes spaghetti and the other dislikes it.

5.9. The mystery of speed

A man walks at a constant speed along the airport. He arrives at a very long corridor. This is equipped with a moving walkway which is running at half of his speed. (Def. moving walkway: Roll bands which work like escalators, but in a straight section). He steps onto this moving walkway and can speed up his walking speed. At the end of the moving walkway, he wants to go back again. He now walks over the moving walkway opposite to the running direction of the moving walkway. Thus, his speed is reduced. Meanwhile, his walking speed is constant. Then, he goes the same distance, with his constant walking speed, forth and back. However, this time he walks next to the moving walkway.
Is the man during the second time going faster, slower or at the same speed compared to the first time with the moving walkway?

5.10. Burglary in the cellar at the barbecue evening

Barbara and Rolf arrange a barbecue in their yard. 9 other people are invited. Among the guests: Alex, Stephanie, the couple Maik and Susi, Tom, Jenny, Frank and another couple, Peter and Laura. Barbecue starts around 3:00 pm. All know each other well, more or less, and quickly become familiar. The evening will go longer than planned which is why Rolf wants to get a fire bowl. However, this is at home in the cellar. He has made the fire bowl recently and has not brought it to the yard yet. Rolf drives home around 8:30 pm, and goes to the cellar. Shocked, he notices that there has been a burglary. The lock is not damaged and the doors were unlocked. Since Rolf has only one key and he had it in the yard, only one of the guests can have stolen his key. The person stole tools, wheels, a radio and an old TV. Rolf is annoyed, because he has canceled his household insurance recently. The timing could not have been worse.

It takes at least three quarters of an hour to go to the apartment, to steal everything and to hide the loot somewhere. On the way back to the yard, Rolf becomes aware that he only trusts Alex blindly. Rolf decides to only tell his wife and Alex about the burglary, and to inquire gradually which guest has an alibi. Maybe, this way he can get the offender.

First, he goes for a walk with Alex and tells him everything. Alex can tell him the following things.
Alex says,
"When we all arrived, we sat at the table and talked extensively. All of us stayed there. Around 4:00 pm, Tom, Jenny and Frank went away. I myself went with Peter and Laura to this patch of forest at 4:30 pm. After we had talked there extensively, we came back around 6:00 pm. Laura went away and Peter stayed with me for a while. I am only sure that Barbara, Peter, Tom and I, we

have been in the yard at 7:00 pm. There we ate salad, drank beer and were looking forward to having a fire. Maik and his wife joined us around 7:30 pm. Then, we stayed in the group until you took me away."

This data does not allow Rolf to identify an offender, yet. He decides to interview Peter. Peter is fully exonerated from Alex's statement which is why he had no reason to lie.
Peter says,
"Mm. I can largely support Alex´s statements. However, I also saw Jenny in the patch of forest. It was around 4:30 pm, when we went there. We met Jenny, Tom and Frank on the way. Certainly, Alex has forgotten this. When I saw the three from a distance, half an hour later, they were standing at a forest ranger stand. It was around 6:00 pm, when Jenny and Barbara prepared the salad. They stood around for a while. Susi, Maik and Tom were with the drinks. After that I was in the yard. "

Rolf cannot make head or tail of the offender. But he can remember that Jenny spent time with him from 7 pm until he drove off. That is why she also cannot be the offender. He asks Jenny as well if she can help him.
Jenny says,
"When I was in the woods, it was 5:00 pm, I watched Stephanie on the phone all the time. She had trouble with her boyfriend. I knew that. When I prepared the salad, she was sitting on the stairs at the entrance. As you and I have been in the yard, she chatted extensively with Frank. I was happy for her, because Frank is a very cute guy and still single. At this evening, they got to know each other a little bit better. Then, the two went for a walk. I saw them again around 8:00 pm."

Rolf remembers that Frank asked him if Stephanie has a boyfriend. That has been about 6:00 pm.

Then, Rolf asks his wife Barbara if she still has few information. Barbara says,
"I talked with Maik and Susi for a while. It was around 5 pm. Afterward, I helped Jenny with the salad. At about 6:30 pm, I met Laura. She also went into the yard, where we were talking with the others. She can't have done it."

Who was not seen for at least one hour?

5.11. The age

How old is Marike?

Marike is 4 years younger than Steffi. Gothold is the oldest man. He is as old as Maik, Tom and Bettina are together. In 4 years, Gothold will be as old as Steffi, Wolfgang and Bernd are together. Tom and Bettina are together 7 years older than Wolfgang. Bernd is 15 years younger than Wolfgang. Susi and Tina are the same age. 4 years ago, Maik was as old as Bettina will be in 15 years. Bettina is 7 years younger than Tom. In 4 years, Wolfgang will be twice as old as Bernd. Susi, Tina and Marike are together as old as Steffi.

5.12. 3 tigers und 3 zebras

3 zebras and 3 tigers stand at a riverbank. All 6 animals have to get to the other side of the river. For this purpose, a raft is available. The raft can carry a maximum of 2 animals. In addition, at least 1 animal has to stand on the raft so that it moves at all. At no shore more tigers than zebras may stand, because these would eat the zebras alive.

Task: Bring the animals - without the tigers eating one of the zebras - to the other side of the river.

5.13. Workplaces

6 old school friends meet and report of past and present. All have become self-employed and run a company. They talk about the number of employees in their respective companies.

Jürgen says,
"I started my company with 7 employees more than Christine did."

Gunther says,
"I have not had changes in the workforce since my third year."

Michael says,
"Now, I have as many employees as Gunther had in his 3rd year."

Christine says,
"All of you have a total of 75 employees today. Congratulations!"

Jürgen says,

"In the 5th year, I had twice as many employees as Christine had in her 5th year."

Gunther says,
"At the beginning, I had as many employees as Christine and Jürgen had together at the start-off of their companies."

Christine says,
"I could hire a new employee annually. This is still the case today."

Heike says,
"Today, Kerstin and I, we would have 21 employees together if I had not fired 5 people."

Kerstin says,
"In my third year, I had as many employees as Jürgen had in his 3rd year. I had to dismiss 4 people to this day."

Jürgen says,
"Until the 5th year, I hired an additional employee annually."

Gunther says,
"The number of my staff has doubled in the first 3 years."

How many employees does Jürgen have today?

5.14. Chaos with the cups

Kristina invites her friends for a cup of coffee. A lot of different cups have accumulated in her coffee cupboard. In order to look neat on the dining table, she needs to sort her cups. For the children, she wants cups that show as many motives as possible. For the adults, she simply tries to find those cups with the pattern which is most available.

Question:
1. How many cups depict most pattern?
2. Cups with which pattern are most available and how many are there?

All cups without circles but with stars, or without stars but with flowers have squares. 3 cups show figures, flowers and squares, and no waves.
6 cups have no stars, but flowers. 4 cups show animals and lines, but no houses, flowers and squares.
The cups with stars but without flowers, have circles. All cups have a circle at the bottom. 5 cups with stars and circles, but without flowers have lines.
All cups with stars but no lines, have waves.
On 2 cups there are no circles and no squares, but figures.
On 4 cups stars and flowers are shown. On 2 cups there are squares, houses and waves. There are 12 cups with stars on it.

5.15. Expenses at purchase

11 female friends have bought new things in the last month.

Question 1: Which woman has spent less and how much did she pay?
Question 2: How much did Martina spent?
Martina spent 100€ less than Maria and Nicole did together.
If Katrin had bought the shoes for 150€, she would have spent as much as Doreen if she herself had not bought the top for 80€.
Maria spent half the amount which Nicole did plus another 35€.
Steffi spent only half the amount of what Doreen did, but also twice of the amount Sophia spent.
Gabi spent 100€ less than Susi did.
Gabi and Susi together spent five times the amount which Katrin spent.
Maria, Nicole and Martina together spent twice the amount which Doreen did. Tina and Gabi spent 750€ together.
Doreen spent three times the amount which Anna did.
Susi spent 100€ less than Tina did.

5.16. The line in the supermarket

A line has formed at the counter in the supermarket. One person pays with credit card. What can you tell about the clothing of this person?

Only one person buys fruit, and thus, healthy fresh food. It is a woman. That is not much, considering that 4 people standing in line. Among them, however, 2 people are male. A person wearing a white shirt, buys cheese. A woman only buys drinks. She has as many products as the other 3 buyers together. The man with the fewest products - he has only 2 things - is relieved that she is not in front of him. The person behind him only buys exactly one product more. The other man stands in front of the woman who only buys drinks and he has only half as many products as she has. One person buys the shopping on credit. That is rare. One woman pays by debit. Only the meat has been paid cash. The person who stands in front of the woman with the fruit buys the meat. One man pays with credit card. Only one person in the line is wearing black shoes. Another person who is not the first in the line is wearing red pants.

6. Miscellaneous

These riddles from different areas of the book require flexible strategies of solution and diverse knowledge of the nature and content of the previous riddles.

6.1. The hardest riddle in the world: "The riddle of columns"

There are 7 columns which stand side by side.
There is information for the following characteristics of the columns:
- the height
- the age
- geometrical characteristics of the basic form
- the color
- the orientation of an arrow at each column
- the symbols of the characters at each column

Task:
The characters are made up of 6 different types of symbols. These are numbers, semicircles, circles, triangles, dots and dashes. Each column shows some of them.

Question:
Which columns all 6 types of symbols are displayed on?

As the requirements of the riddle are extremely high, the first trials are likely to end up with a false result. So in order to not get to know the solution right away, but nevertheless gain a way of checking, please proceed as follows.

1. Consecutively, number the columns from left to right with 1-7 (i.e. position code).
2. Write the number of the symbols of the respective column below the position code.
3. Multiply the two numbers and record the result.
4. Summate the 7 calculated results.
5. The result is the check digit.
6. Check digit: 132

Example:

column	1	2	3	4	5	6	7
number	3	1	6	2	4	1	3
product	3	2	18	8	20	6	21

Digit: 78

Hint: Of course, there are other combinations of the results which yield to this check digit. If your digit is correct, please, look to the solution part, finally.

1. Square columns show dots as characters.
2. Next to the brown column, there is a column whose arrow points to the southwest and that depicts dashes as characters.
3. A column with a height of 190 cm, is 10,300 years old.
4. 4 columns have the same height.
5. To the left of the oldest column, there is the orange column which shows circles.
6. All columns together have a total length of 54 m.
7. The column which is 400 years older than the column in the middle, stands to the left of that column which is 200 cm wide.
8. The 9,000-year-old column shows the number three, dashes, circles, triangles and an arrow to the west.
9. To the left of the gray column which shows numbers, there stands the dark green column.
10. The column with a width of 190 cm shows triangles as characters and an arrow pointing to the southwest.
11. The 2 smallest columns stand side by side and show circles as characters.
12. The column with the arrow pointing south stands to the left of the column which shows an arrow pointing east.
13. A column has a diameter of 225 cm, has dashes, dots, triangles and circles as characters, and is 9,300 years old.
14 To the right of the middle column, there stands a three-times-higher column.
15. The column with the smallest diameter shows a numerical series.
16. The white column which is 8,900 years old shows triangles.
17. Between 2 square columns there is always a round column.
18. The second-left column, starting from the light green column is 205 cm wide, and shows semicircles as characters.
19. The columns with a width of 200 cm and 230 cm are side by side and have semicircles and triangles as a character.
20. The light green column is 300 years younger than the neighboring column, shows semicircles and is 210 cm wide.

21. The 9,900-year-old column is precisely 400 years younger than the second-left, and shows numbers and dashes.
22. The rectangular-shape of the column with a width of 205 cm has a circumference of 1,010 cm.
23. To the right of the column which shows an eastern arrow, there is a column showing a south-eastern arrow.
24. Adding up the depth of all 4 square columns, we obtain a distance of 11 m.
25. The highest column has a width of 205 cm and dashes as characters.
26. The light yellow column stands next to the column which shows an arrow to the west.
27. The first two columns are the same height and have a length of 18 m all together.
28. The round column that is the closest to the brown column is 800 years older than the second-right one.
29. The column which has only half the height of the middle column looks like a geometric cube.
30. The column with the highest depth is not gray, shows dots and triangles as a character, and does not point to the northwest.
31. To the right of the north-east arrow, the round column shows a north arrow and numbers.
32. Diameter and width of two adjacent columns have the same length: 190 cm.

6.2. Text and numbers

Solve this number block.
All solution numbers are between 0 and 7.
"Neighbor" means numbers which are directly adjacent.

	numbers < 5 & exisiting not more than twice	neighbors difference of 1	neighbors difference of 1	numbers < 4	no number exists twice	each number exisits three times	
every number exists once							every number exists once
even numbers, in pairs							every number exists twice
neighbors are unequal							odd numbers
every number exists once							every number exists once
numbers >2							2 neighbors are identical twice
every number exists once							every number exists once
	neighbors are different	neighbors difference of 1	each number exisits once	neighbors difference of 1	no number exists four times	each number exisits three times	

6.3. Number blocks

Fill out the empty fields.
Note: Look at the blocks as a whole.

1	2	3	4
6	4	4	3
11	8	1	2
		58	1

3	4		6
	8	1	5
11	16	5	4
15	32	15	3

5			8
8	12	1	
11	24	1	
14	48	-23	5

7	8	9	10
		14	
	32	11	
13	64		

6.4. Logic

Find the right logical conclusion. In fact, not all of the premises are correct. Concerning the conclusions, only the statements of the premises are important. So, the logical value is secondary.

It is biologically proven that all dogs are mammals. That is a fact. Furthermore, it is certain that no mammal is not a warm-blooded animal. The correlation is quite interesting considering that no mammal hibernates. These also include some fish, because these are also mammals. There is also no bird, which is a mammal. Frogs belong to the amphibian. There is also no frog which is not a carnivore. The world of fish is interesting. There are some fish which are not mammals. For many people it is surprising that not all fish are not mammals. For cats, that is different. There is no cat which is not a mammal. In addition, all cats are carnivores.

The following conclusions can be selected:

1. All birds are warm-blooded.
2. All birds are not fish.
3. Some fish suckle their young.
4. Birds do not hibernate.
5. Some carnivores are not cats.
6. Some amphibians are not carnivores.

6.5. Complete the task

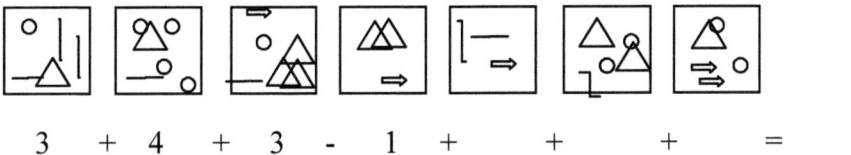

3 + 4 + 3 - 1 + __ + __ + __ = __

6.6. Which city are we looking for?
Note: The city has 4 letters and it is a German word.

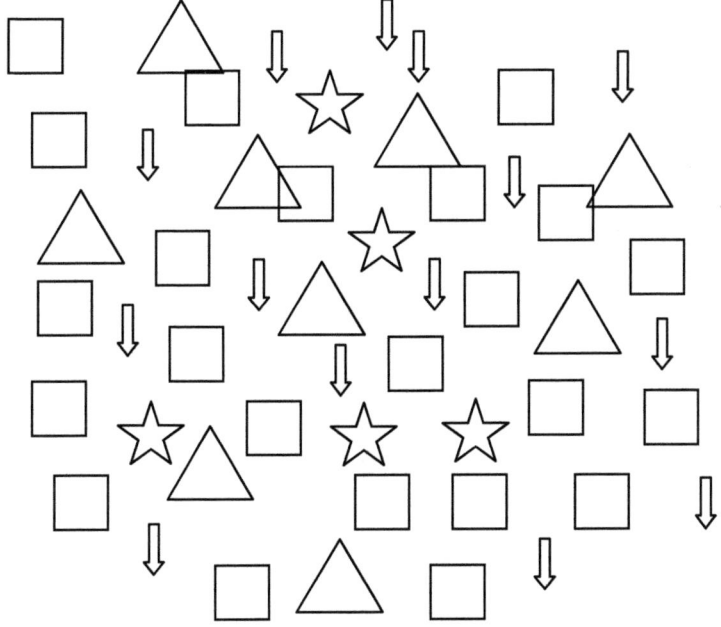

6.7. Find the city.

The rule, "multiplication and division first, then addition and subtraction" is omitted in this task.

4	+		+		=	33
+		-		+		
	+		-	6	=	11
/		/		-		
5	*	5	-		=	6
=		=		=		
4	+	10	-	5	=	

6.8. Spaceships and the light

Some spaceships fly alongside a light beam. Each one has a different speed. The beam itself moves with its known 300,000 km/s (rounded value). The white spaceship flies with 80,000 km/s along the light beam. In respect to the yellow spaceship, the white one flies 10,000 km/s. The red spaceship flies about 20,000 km/s faster than the green spaceship. From the perspective of the green space ship, the yellow spaceship flies 20,000 km/s slower. The blue spaceship has twice the speed of the yellow spaceship. The blue spaceship overtakes the gray one with 40,000 km/s. Measured from the brown spaceship, the red spaceship flies 30,000 km/s. The black spaceship overtakes the green spaceship with 40,000 km/s. But the black spaceship is still 40,000 km/s slower than the orange spaceship.
What speed (of the light beam) does the crew of the orange spaceship measure?

6.9. The age

Bernd turned 30 years last week. His sister is 5 years younger. His old army friend is three years older than the sister of Bernd. Markus, Bernd's longtime friend, is 3 years older than Bernd. At least, this was like that 2 weeks ago. He always had a heart for Sophia. The teacher, from the training of Markus, is as old as Markus and Sophia are together. Coincidentally, the teacher and the father of Markus went to school together, formerly. However, Markus' father was sent to school one year earlier, which is why he is one year older. Incidentally, it was also his father who gave his sister Sophia her name. The old army friend of Bernd is now married to a woman who is 5 years older than himself.
15 years ago, Markus' mother was half as old as the father of Sophia is nowadays. His mother is a housewife now. Just like Beate (the partner of the old army friend) has become since 6 months. She is expecting a child. Unfortunately, the mother of Markus has never settled down in the professional world again, as she has been dismissed 4 years ago. However, Beate hopes that she can get back to work one year after childbirth.

What age the mother of Sophia was dismissed at?

Solution part:
Always cover the following lines with a sheet of paper if you use the solution part.

Solution:
1.1.1. Result: 1.99 cm
1.1.2. Result: 6.38 cm
1.1.3. Result: 2.69 cm
1.1.4. Result: 12.56 cm
1.1.5. Result: 112.25 cm
1.1.6. Result: 10 cm
1.1.7. Result: 63.13 cm
1.1.8. Result: 36.06 cm
1.1.9. Result: 26.40 cm
1.1.10. Result: 4.89 cm
(Pythagoras´ theorem)
1.2.1. Result: 12.78 cm
1.2.2. Result: 4.60 cm
1.2.3. Result: 0.67 cm
1.2.4. Result: 12.48 cm
1.2.5. Result: 4.87 cm
1.2.6. Result: 6.86 cm (Note: Euclid´s altitude theorem: $h^2=x*(8.28-x)$)
1.2.7. Result: 5.80 cm
1.2.8. Result: 9.29 cm
1.2.9. Result: 6.20 cm
1.2.10. Result: 6.84 cm
(Intercept theorems, all theorems in a right triangle)
1.3.1. Result: 3.25 cm
1.3.2. Result: 3.81 cm
1.3.3. Result: 10.47 cm
1.3.4. Result: 10.66 cm
1.3.5. Result: 10.68 cm
1.3.6. Result: 16.98 cm
1.3.7. Result: 24.36 cm
1.3.8. Result: 5.53 cm
1.3.9. Result: 2.6 cm
1.3.10. Result: 22.14 cm
(golden section, theorems on circle)

2.1.1.
Hint: You will recognize most residents if you search for all information about the residents in the text.

	1	2	3	4
color	brown	**green**	white	yellow
residents	6	3	5	2
car brand	VW	Audi	Peugeot	Mazda

2.1.2.

	1	2	3	4
steps	10	8	14	2
windows	9	13	6	**10**
children	none	2	4	1

2.1.3.

	1	2	3	4
nationality	German	Dutchman	Italian	Frenchman
color	white	gray	black	**red**
house's age	20 years	110 years	10 years	30 years

2.1.4.

	1	2	3	4
profession	teacher	mechanician	electrician	**hairdresser**
car brand	VW	Seat	Porsche	Volvo
house's age	5 years	16 years	43 years	20 years

2.1.5.

	1	2	3	4
house's color	yellow	brown	light blue	gray
border	wall	fence	hedge	lattice
cellar/loft	**yes / yes**	no / yes	no / no	yes / no

2.1.6.

	1	2	3	4
yard	2 yards	none/small	big	none/small
house's color	**dark green**	yellow	gray	orange
car's color	black	red	white	gray

2.1.7.

	1	2	3	4
house's age	45 years	**130 years**	50 years	8 years
windows	6	5	15	12
children	1	3	5	2

2.1.8.

	1	2	3	4
yard	3	1	none	2
steps	**12**	2	4	6
car brand	Mercedes	VW	Peugeot	Fiat

2.1.9.

	1	2	3	4
pet	**mouse**	cat	dog	bird
children	2	4	1	3
nationality	Italian	Spaniard	Finn/Swiss	Finn/Swiss

2.1.10.

	1	2	3	4
profession	hairdresser	trainer	official	policeman
border	wall	fence	none	hedge
house's age	**10**	14	70	34

2.2.1.
Hint1: First, regard the age.
Hint2: If the 4 owners are 41.5 years old in average, all together are 166 years old. The age of the fourth can be calculated.

	1	2	3	4
age	40	youngest (38)	46	42
size	188cm	182cm (-6cm H1)	181cm	191 cm
house's color	white	brown	gray	green
car brand	**Audi**	VW	Opel	Fiat

2.2.2.
Hint1: Start with the house's color.
Hint2: The question contains information, too.

	1	2	3	4
plot	800 m²	1,200 m²	950 m²	1500 m²
children	**2**	4	1	3
house's age	10	15	45	31
house's color	green	red	gray	white

2.2.3.

	1	2	3	4
profession	baker	painter	businessman	electrician
pasta/pizza	+ / +	- / -	+ / -	- / +
age	**43**	35	27 (-8 H2)	51 (+24 H3)
car brand	Volvo	Seat	BMW	Opel

2.2.4.

	1	2	3	4
pet	cat	bird	fish	hamster
children	1	0	3	2
size	187 cm	167 cm (-20 H1)	191 cm	188 cm
age	43 (-2 H3)	51	45	**49**

2.2.5.

	1	2	3	4
value	250	180	120,000	150
windows	**6**	8	14	10 (-4 H3)
steps	4	5	2	7
color	gray	green	brown	white
age	40	20	80	50

2.2.6.

	1	2	3	4
pet	fish	dog	hamster	bird
soccer/hand b	+/-	-/-	-/+	+/+
apples/plums	-/-	+/-	-/+	+/+
hobby	hockey	chess	riddle	**car**
profession	businessman	mechanician	veterinarian	agent

2.2.7.
Hint: For each house, you can deduce the age of the owner/house from the age of the house/owner.

	1	2	3	4
children	3	1 (-1 H4)	5 (+3 H4)	2
car´s color	**gray**	yellow	blue	white
car brand	VW	Opel	Renault	BMW
age	49	40	57	48
house´s age	51	60	43	52

2.8.

	1	2	3	4
smoking/drink	+ / -	- / -	- / +	+ / +
age	45	**35**	41	49
profession	hairdresser	trainer	mechanician	agent
hair color	blond	black	brown	red
skat/poker	- / -	+ / +	+ / -	- / +

2.2.9.

	1	2	3	4
age	32	35	41	55
size	182	175	189	190
plot	150	210	160	190
profession	businessman	teacher	driver	**author**
car brand	Fiat	BMW	Porsche	Seat

2.2.10.
Hint: If you know the difference of two values of 2 parties, you can possibly relate to the values from the text.

	1	2	3	4
border	wall	fence	hedge	fir tree
size	190 cm	181 cm	185 cm	187 cm
income	2,1	3,4	1,3	2,8
age	34	(+7 H1) 41	29	38
house´s age	**12**	70	(-15 H4) 45	60

2.3.1.
Hint: Start with the number of children.

	1	2	3	4	5
children	4	1	3	2	6
car brand	VW	Audi	BMW	Renault	Opel
house´s color	green	gray	yellow	white	brown
hair color	blond	**black**	gray	red	brown
age	34	51	63	40	44
rice/pasta/potatoes	+ / - / +	+ / + / -	- / - / +	- / + / -	+ / - / -

2.3.2.
Hint1: Start with the income. Not all numbers have to be found in the text to make an unambiguous assignment possible.
Hint2: The names will tell you if somebody is male or female. Please, note this in the statements.

	1	2	3	4	5
income	4,1	3,6	3,2	2,5	2,85
name	**Beate**	Steffen	Marika	Susi	Maik
cycle/jog/swim	+ / - / +	+ / + / +	- / - / +	+ / - / -	- / + / -
age	43	51(+21H 3)	30	42	29
profession	saleslady	agent	female caregiver	female attorney	craftsman
car's color	yellow	brown	black	gray	green

2.3.3.
Hint: Start with the cars.

	1	2	3	4	5
car brand	**VW**	Opel	BMW	Fiat	Mercedes
car's color	black	white		brown	gray
house's color	white	orange	green	brown	gray
hair color	blond	brown/black	brown/black	bald head	red
hobby	riddle	cards	stamps	climbing	motorcycle
profession	trainer	trader	agent	business man	mechanician

2.3.4.
Hint: Start with the drinks.

	1	2	3	4	5	6
profession	**teacher**	baker	salesclerk	agent	butcher	glazier
age	45	51	34	31	50	26
car	Opel	Porsche	Fiat	Peugeot	VW	Audi
house´s color	yellow	orange	white	brown	green	red
drink	juice	milk	coffee	tea	water/cocoa	water/cocoa
food	spaghetti	potato salad	bockw.	steak	salad	hamb.

2.3.5.
Hint: Start with the age.

	1	2	3	4	5
name	Martin	Kerstin	Sophia	**Steffi**	Hans
age	65	51	43	46	52
house´s age	70	15	42	50	43
pizza/Salad/fruit	- / - / +	+ / + / +	- / + / -	+ / - / +	+ / + / -
shop/hike/fly	- / - / -	+ / - / +	+ / + / -	- / + / +	- / + / -
size	181	171	173	165	189

2.3.6.

	1	2	3	4	5
name	Beate	Tim	Rolf	Tina	Maria
profession	female kindergarden teacher	electrician	doctor	female attorney	policewoman
hobby	skiing	cycling	music	**jogging**	
handb/hockey/volleyball	+ / - / -	+ / - / +	- / - / -	+ / + / -	+ / + / +
car´s color	green	yellow	black	brown	red
rice/fish/beef/bread	+ / + / - / -	- / - / - / +	- / + / + / +	+ / + / + / -	- / + / - / +

2.3.7.

Hint: Start with the name. There is only one man living on one side completely external.

	1	2	3	4	5	6
name	Stefanie	Tobias	Martina	**Kerstin**	Ulf	Markus
read/TV/ PC/draw	+ / + / - / +	- / + / + / +	+ / - / + / +	- / - / + / -	+ / + / + / -	+ / - / + / -
size	172	181	167	177	186	191
income	1,8	1,9	2,3	2,1	1,5	2,8
profession	saleslady	technician	female teacher	female principal	craftsman	smith
hair color	green	black	blond	red	brown	bald head

2.3.8.

	1	2	3	4	5	6
windows	12	14	8	9	15	7
smokes	Pall M.	Cabinet	West	F6	Marlboro	Davidoff
reads	Non-fiction books	Crime books	poems	short stories	dramas	magazines
sports	Hockey/ soccer	Hockey/ soccer	tennis		volleyb.	sailing
age	45	61	**53**	50	57	41
nation	French man	English	Swiss	German	Spaniard	Italian

2.3.9.
Hint: If you do not know anything about a house, there cannot be a information/solution this way. (that is why house 1 cannot be brown, because there is no information about the income.)

	1	2	3	4	5	6
age	56	43	+10H6 (51)		66	-25H5 (41)
income		2,7	2			1,8
size		-H5(181)	177	+5H5(193)	188	
name	Bernd	Maik		Wolfgang	Eberhard	Michael
car brand		Renault	BMW	Opel	Fiat	VW
house´s color		yellow/white	orange	yellow/white	red	brown

2.3.10.

	1	2	3	4	5	6
nation	**Swede**	Finn	Dane	Swiss	Hungarian	Spaniard
hobby	soccer	Ski	handball/climbing	handball/climbing	flying	
profession	carpenter	roofer	mechanician	agent	brick layer	technician
learned	clerk		salesclerk	driver		electrician
food	French fries	fish	rice/pasta	rice/pasta	ice cream	chocolate
pet	cat	dog	bird		hamster	rat

3.1.1.
4(+3) 7(-2) 5(+3) 8(-2) 6 **9 7 10**
3.1.2.
-5(-8) -13(-4) -17(+2) -15(-8) -23 **-27 -25 -33**
3.1.3.
15(+6) 21(-1) 20(-3) 17(+6) 23 **22 19 25**
3.1.4.
5(+18) 23(+4) 27(+1) 28(+18) 46 **50 51 69**
3.1.5.

-45(+4) -41(-8) -49(-3) -52(+4) -48 **-56 -59 -55**
3.1.6.
10(+4) 14(-5) 9(+4) 13(-6) 7(+4) 11(-5) 6 **10 4 8**
3.1.7.
40(-2) 38(-19) 19(-2) 17(-19) -2 **-4 -23 -25**
3.1.8.
8(-2) 6(-2) 4(+4) 8(-2) 6 **4 8 6**
3.1.9.
14(-7) 7(-4) 3(-7) -4(+1) -3(-7) -10(-4) -14 **-21 -20 -27**
3.1.10.
5(-4) 1(+3) 4(-4) 0 **3 -1 2**
3.1.11.
11(+11) 22(+11) 33(-3) 30(+11) 41 **52 49 60**
3.1.12.
31(+4) 35(+6) 41(+5) 46(+4) 50 **56 61 65**
3.1.13.
7(+5) 12(-3) 9(-2) 7(-1) 6(+5) 11 **8 6 5**
3.1.14.
15(-5) 10(-5) 5(-5) 0(+1) 1(-5) -4 **-9 -14 -13**
3.1.15.
113(-8) 105(+3) 108(+2) 110(-8) 102 **105 107 99**
3.1.16.
-55(-15) -70(-10) -80(-5) -85(-15) -100 **-110 -115 -130**
3.1.17.
-14(+4) -10(+1) -9(-3) -12(-2) -14(+4) -10 **-9 -12 -14**
3.1.18.
(The summand is sequentially always smaller by 1.)
13(+12) 25(+11) 36(+10) 46(+9) 55 **63 70 76**
3.1.19.
0(+5) 5(-6) -1(+3) 2(-6) -4(+5) 1 **-5 -2 -8**
3.1.20.
9(-6) 3(-3) 0(+3) 3(-6) -3 **-6 -3 -9**
3.2.
Note: In order to recognize a sequence of numbers, at least the last arithmetic operation of the given sequence of numbers has to be identical to the first. So perhaps, conclusions can result from the first sequence of numbers.
3.2.1.
4(*6) 24(/3) 8(+18) 26(-20) 6(*6) 36(/3) 12 **30 10 60**
3.2.2.
15(/5) 3(*10) 30(+5) 35(/5) 7(*10) 70 **75 15 150**

3.2.3.
14(*3) 42(*-2) -84 (*-3) 252(*2) 504(*3) 1512 **-3024 9072 18144**
3.2.4.
3(-6) -3(*2) -6(+8) 2(-5) -3(-6) -9 **-18 -10 -15**
3.2.5.
2(*5) 10(-1) 9(*5) 45(+2) 47(*5) 235(-1) 234 **1170 1172 5860**
3.2.6.
7(-4) 3(*-2) -6(*0) 0(-4) -4(*-2) 8(*0) 0 **-4 8 0**
3.2.7.
2(-10) -8(/2) -4(-6) -10(-10) -20(/2) -10 **-16 -26 -13**
3.2.8.
0(-4) -4(-5) -9(+8) -1(+6) 5(-4) 1 **-4 4 10**
3.2.9.
3(*-1) -3(+5) 2(-7) -5(+11) 6(*-1) -6 **-1 -8 3**
3.2.10.
16(/4) 4(-7) -3(+4) 1(+3) 4(/4) 1 **-6 -2 1**
3.2.11.
10(/2) 5(*3) 15(-17) -2(/2) -1(*3) -3 **-20 -10 -30**
3.2.12.
13(-7) 6(*-4) -24(+18) -6(+7) 1(-7) -6(*-4) 24 **42 49 42**
3.2.13.
3(*-3) -9(*2) -18(+6) -12(*-3) 36(*2) 72 **78 -234 -468**
3.2.14.
-3(-12) -15(+10) -5(-3) -8(+10) 2(-12) -10 **0 -3 7**
3.2.15.
13(*0) 0(+5) 5(*0) +0(-2) -2(*0) 0 **5 0 -2**
3.2.16.
4(*3) 12(*2) 24(-18) 6(*3) 18 **36 18 54**
3.2.17.
-13(*2) -26(+4) -22(+25) 3(*2) 6(+4) 10(+25) 35 **70 74 99**
3.2.18.
-17(*-2) 34(-30) 4(-7) -3(*-2) 6 **-24 -31 62**
3.2.19.
7(*-1) -7(*2) -14(*-1) 14(*2) 28 **-28 -56 56**
3.2.20.
30(-24) 6(-8) -2(+10) 8(-24) -16 **-24 -14 -38**
3.3.1.
Alternately, add and subtract prime numbers.
4(+2) 6(-3) 3(+5) 8(-7) 1(+11) 12 **-1 16 -3**
3.3.2.
Multiply even numbers and add odd numbers.

-6(+1) -5(*2) -10(+3) -7(*4) -28 **-23 -138 -131**
3.3.3.
4(+8) 12(-5) 7(*3) 21(+8) 29(-5) 24(*3) 72 **80 75 225**
3.3.4.
Add prime numbers and subtract the remaining odd numbers.
-20(-1) -21(+2) -19(+3) -16(+5) -11(+7) -4(-9) -13 **-2 11 -4**
3.3.5.
Add up two consecutive even numbers and subtract the following odd number.
-10(+2) -8(+4) -4(-5) -9(+6) -3(+8) 5 **-4 6 18**
3.3.6.
The sequence of prime numbers.
17 19 23 29 31 37 **41 43 47**
3.3.7.
Add and subtract consecutive even numbers, alternately. After two numbers, the result will be multiplied by 3.
1(+2) 3(-4) -1(*3) -3(+6) 3(-8) -5(*3) -15 **-5 -17 -51**
3.3.8.
3(*2) 6(-3) 3(-5) -2(*4) -8(-6) -14(-10) -24(*2) -48 **-51 -56 -224**
3.3.9.
3(*4) 12(/2) 6(*3) 18(-5) 13(*4) 52 **26 78 73**
3.3.10.
41(+1) 42(+3) 45(-2) 43(-4) 39(-1) 38(-3) 35(+2) 37(+4) 41(+1) 42 **45 43 39**
3.3.11.
Add odd numbers of the sequence of numbers and multiply even numbers.
3(+1) 4(*2) 8(+3) 11(*4) 44(+5) 49 **294 301 2408**
3.3.12.
Add the multiples of three, successively.
5(+3) 8(+6) 14(+9) 23(+12) 35 **50 68 89**
3.3.13.
The consecutive prime numbers are added twice and subtracted once.
-31(+2) -29(+3) -26(-5) -31(+7) -24(+11) -13(-13) -26(+17) -9 **10 -13 16**
3.3.14.
-7(+3) -4(+5) 1(+3) 4(-5) -1(-3) -4(-5) -9(+3) -6 **-1 2 -3**
3.3.15.
-2(*2) -4(*2) -8(+3) -5(*2) -10(*2) -20(+3) -17 **-34 -68 -65**
3.3.16.
Consecutive even numbers are added in pairs and then subtracted in pairs.
5(+2) 7(+4) 11(-6) 5(-8) -3(+10) 7 **19 5 -11**
3.3.17.

Of a sequence of numbers, even numbers are subtracted and odd numbers are multiplied.
5(-4) 1(*5) 5(-6) -1(*7) -7(-8) -15(*9) -135 **-145 -1595 -1607**
3.3.18.
Consecutive prime numbers are subtracted.
4(-2) 2(-3) -1(-5) -6(-7) -13(-11) -24 **-37 -54 -73**
3.3.19.
-3(*-2) 6(*-3) -18(-5) -23(*-2) 46(*-3) -138 **-143 286 -858**
3.3.20.
Prime numbers are added and the remaining odd numbers are substracted.
-35(-1) -36(+2) -34(+3) -31(+5) -26(+7) -19(-9) -28(+11) -17 **-4 -19 -2**
3.4.1.
Add up continuously. The summand is in turn made up of the sum of the positive sequence of numbers.
1(+1) 2(+1+2) 5(+1+2+3) 11(+1+2+3+4) 21 **36 57 85**
3.4.2.
Multiply the number with their sum of the digits.
11(*2) 22(+4) 88(*16) 1408(*13) 18304 **292864**
3.4.3.
Keep adding. The summands are the predecessors and successors of consecutive positive numbers.
-45(Zahl2: 1;3) -44, -41(Zahl3: 2;4) -39, -35(Zahl 4: 3;5) -32 -27 **-23 -17 -12 -5**
3.4.4.
The solutions are the sums of digits of consecutive prime numbers.
2(2) 3(3) 5(5) 7(7) 2(1+1) 4(1+3) 8(1+7) **10 5 11**
3.4.5.
Always subtract twice the consecutive prime numbers.
4(-4) 0(-6) -6(-10) -16(-14) -30 **-52 -78 -112**
3.4.6.
The sum of three consecutive numbers always is 35. For each block, the first number is reduced by 1 and the second number is reduced by 2, and to compensate, add 3 to the third number.
15+12+8= 35 / 14+10+11= 35 / 13+8+14=35 / **12 6 17**
3.4.7.
The consecutive prime numbers are added and then subtracted. The result is squared in the third step.
4(+2) 6(-3) 3(^{2}) 9(+5) 14(-7) 7(^{2}) 49(+11) 60(-13) 47(^{2}) 2209 **2226 2207**
3.4.8.

In the first step, multiply by -3, and then add 4. In the third step, the sum of digits is added up again.
2(*-3) -6(+4) -2(+2) 0(*-3) 0(+4) 4(+4) 8(*-3) -24(+4) -20(+2) -18(*-3) 54(+4) 58 (+13) 71 **-213 -209 -198**
3.4.9.
Consecutive odd numbers are added up. Every second even number is subtracted. Always do this alternately.
0(+1) 1(-2) -1(+3) 2(-6) -4(+5) 1(-10) -9(+7) -2(-14) -16 **-7 -25 -14**
3.4.10.
It is a sequence of numbers made by four steps. The first two arithmetic operations are performed with summands which are steadily – starting with 3 – doubled. In the third step, substract 4, and in the fourth step, subtract 1.
1(+3) 4(+6) 10(-4) +6(-1) 5(+12) 17(+24) 41(-4) 37(-1) 36 **84 180 176**
3.4.11.
All odd numbers – starting with 11 – are used. Prime numbers are subtracted and the remaining odd numbers are added up.
10(-11) -1(-13) -14(+15) 1(-17) -16(-19) -35 **-14 -37 -12**
3.4.12.
The odd numbers are subtracted and run from 21 downwards. The even numbers are added up and start with 4.
-3(-21) -24(+4) -20(-19) -39(+6) -33(-17) -50(+8) -42 **-57 -47 -60**
3.4.13.
Add twice and subtract once. The numbers run from 4 backwards, including zero and negative numbers.
-8(+4) -4(+3) -1(-2) -3(+1) -2 **-2 -1 -3 -6**
3.4.14.
The numbers come in pairs always to the sum of 19. The two summands are arbitrarily chosen.
(13+6)19, (10+9) 19, (8+**11**)19
3.4.15.
-2(+3) 1(-2) -1(-1) -2(-3) -5(+4) -1(-6) -7(+3) -4 **-6 -7 -10 -6 -12**
3.4.16.
There are always four steps. In the first and second step, the prime numbers are continuously added. At the beginning of the new series, these simply continue counting. In the third step, multiply by 3 and in the fourth step, subtract 10.
0(+2) 2(+3) 5(*3) 15(-10) 5(+5) 10(+7) 17(*3) 51(-10) 41 **52 65 195 185 202**
3.4.17.
Continuously multiply the prime numbers and always add 1 to the result.
3(*2+1) 7(*3+1) 22(*5+1) 111 **778 8559**

3.4.18.
Each three-block adds up to 40. The first and second number is always added by 3 per block. The third number is subtracted by 6.
(17+15+8=40) (20+18+2=40) (23+21-4=40) **(26+24-10=40)**
3.4.19.
First, multiply twice and then add twice. This procedure just continues. The value simply runs continuously.
-4(*2) -8(*3) -24(+4) -20(+5) -15(*6) -90(*7) -630(+8) -622(+9) -613 -**6130 -67430 -67418 -67405**
3.4.20.
There are four steps. In the first step, multiply by 4 and in the second step, by 3. In the third step, divide by 2. In the fourth step, even numbers are continuously added up. Therefore, per step always 2 more.
2(*4) 8(*3) 24(/2) 12(+2) 14(*4) 56(*3) 168(/2) 84(+4) 88 **352 1056 528**

4.1.1.

4	x	3	=	12
x		+		
6	-	5	=	1
=		=		
24		8		

4.1.2.

14	-	8	=	6
+		x		
3	x	5	=	15
=		=		
17		40		

4.1.3.

21	/	3	=	7
-		+		
8	x	5	=	40
=		=		
13		8		

4.1.4.

9	x	3	=	27
+		-		
8	x	2	=	16
=		=		
17		1		

4.1.5.

6	x	2	=	12
+		+		
5	+	7	=	12
=		=		
11		9		

4.1.6.

5	x	4	=	20
+		/		
3	-	1	=	2
=		=		
8		4		

4.1.7.

16	/	4	=	4
-		x		
11	+	3	=	14
=		=		
5		12		

4.1.8.

3	+	10	=	13
x		/		
5	-	2	=	3
=		=		
15		5		

4.1.9.

12	/	4	=	3
-		x		
6	+	5	=	11
=		=		
6		20		

4.1.10.

9	/	3	=	3
-		x		
4	+	6	=	10
=		=		
5		18		

4.1.11.

14	-	10	=	4
/		+		
2	x	6	=	12
=		=		
7		16		

4.1.12.

6	+	11	=	17
x		x		
5	-	2	=	3
=		=		
30		22		

4.1.13.

6	+	6	=	12
+		x		
12	-	2	=	10
=		=		
18		12		

4.1.14.

8	+	3	=	11
-		x		
4	+	7	=	11
=		=		
4		21		

4.1.15.

5	+	15	=	20
x		-		
2	+	7	=	9
=		=		
10		8		

4.1.16.

7	+	6	=	13
+		x		
6	-	5	=	1
=		=		
13		30		

4.1.17.

8	/	8	=	1
/		+		
2	x	7	=	14
=		=		
4		15		

4.1.18.

1	+	13	=	14
x		-		
7	-	6	=	1
=		=		
7		7		

4.1.19.

13	-	9	=	4
x		/		
1	+	3	=	4
=		=		
13		3		

4.1.20.

16	/	2	=	8
/		x		
4	+	4	=	8
=		=		
4		8		

4.2.1.

6	/	3	+	18	=	20
x		x		-		
3	+	7	-	3	=	7
+		-		/		
2	+	8	/	5	=	2
=		=		=		
20		13		3		

4.2.2.

9	+	3	/	4	=	3
/		x		+		
3	+	8	x	2	=	22
+		/		-		
7	x	2	-	5	=	9
=		=		=		
10		12		1		

4.2.3.

15	/	5	x	6	=	18
/		+		x		
3	+	7	/	2	=	5
x		/		-		
5	+	4	x	2	=	18
=		=		=		
5		3		10		

4.2.4.

20	/	10	x	5	=	10
/		x		+		
4	+	3	+	6	=	13
+		/		-		
3	x	6	/	9	=	2
=		=		=		
8		5		2		

4.2.5.

19	+	2	/	3	=	7
-		x		+		
4	x	4	-	6	=	10
/		-		/		
5	+	7	/	3	=	4
=		=		=		
3		1		3		

4.2.6.

5	x	7	-	21	=	14
x		+		/		
6	/	2	+	7	=	10
-		/		x		
7	+	3	+	5	=	15
=		=		=		
23		3		15		

4.2.7.

7	+	5	x	2	=	24
-		+		+		
4	x	3	-	10	=	2
x		/		-		
6	/	2	+	8	=	11
=		=		=		
18		4		4		

4.2.8.

11	+	10	/	7	=	3
+		+		x		
4	+	16	-	8	=	12
/		+		-		
5	+	16	-	20	=	1
=		=		=		
3		42		36		

4.2.9.

31	+	2	/	3	=	11
-		+		x		
11	+	5	/	4	=	4
/		+		-		
2	x	7	+	7	=	21
=		=		=		
10		14		5		

4.2.10.

20	+	15	/	7	=	5
-		-		+		
14	x	3	/	6	=	7
+		-		-		
3	x	5	-	10	=	5
=		=		=		
9		7		3		

4.2.11.

18	+	12	/	6	=	5
x		+		+		
2	+	13	+	7	=	22
/		/		+		
9	x	5	-	12	=	33
=		=		=		
4		5		25		

4.2.12.

15	+	15	/	6	=	5
x		-		+		
3	x	8	-	16	=	8
/		x		/		
5	x	6	-	11	=	19
=		=		=		
9		42		2		

4.2.13.

17	+	3	+	3	=	23
-		+		x		
10	-	8	x	9	=	18
x		-		+		
4	+	7	x	3	=	33
=		=		=		
28		4		30		

4.2.14.

30	/	5	+	13	=	19
-		x		+		
20	-	4	x	2	=	32
+		-		-		
15	+	6	/	7	=	3
=		=		=		
25		14		8		

4.2.15.

9	+	13	+	31	=	53
x		+		-		
6	+	5	-	4	=	7
-		/		/		
15	/	3	+	9	=	14
=		=		=		
39		6		3		

4.2.16.

14	x	3	-	15	=	27
+		+		-		
32	/	4	+	7	=	15
/		/		+		
23	-	7	/	8	=	2
=		=		=		
2		1		16		

4.2.17.

56	/	2	/	7	=	4
/		+		-		
8	+	9	-	4	=	13
+		x		x		
13	-	3	+	7	=	17
=		=		=		
20		33		21		

4.2.18.

15	-	5	/	5	=	2
+		+		x		
9	+	11	x	3	=	60
/		/		-		
8	x	4	+	7	=	39
=		=		=		
3		4		8		

4.2.19.

17	+	8	/	5	=	5
+		/		+		
7	+	4	+	7	=	18
/		x		x		
3	+	13	-	3	=	13
=		=		=		
8		26		36		

4.2.20.

32	-	30	x	7	=	14
/		/		+		
2	+	10	x	1	=	12
+		+		/		
5	x	8	/	4	=	10
=		=		=		
21		11		2		

4.3.1.

12	+	14	/	2	-	10	=	3
x		/		+		-		
3	x	2	+	5	+	5	=	16
-		+		-		+		
10	+	8	/	6	x	7	=	21
/		+		x		/		
2	+	5	+	2	/	3	=	3
=		=		=		=		
13		20		2		4		

4.3.2.

44	-	34	x	3	/	5	=	6
/		/		+		+		
11	+	2	+	5	/	9	=	2
+		-		/		-		
7	+	3	-	4	x	3	=	18
x		/		+		+		
2	+	7	/	3	+	8	=	11
=		=		=		=		
22		2		5		19		

4.3.3.

18	x	3	-	30	/	8	=	3
/		+		-		/		
9	+	5	/	7	+	4	=	6
+		x		-		x		
7	x	4	-	15	+	7	=	20
x		-		/		+		
3	x	10	/	2	+	6	=	21
=		=		=		=		
27		22		4		20		

4.3.4.

32	-	12	x	2	/	8	=	5
/		/		+		+		
8	/	4	x	8	+	9	=	25
+		+		+		+		
6	+	9	/	5	x	7	=	21
/		x		/		/		
5	-	3	x	3	x	4	=	24
=		=		=		=		
2		36		5		6		

4.3.5.

14	-	10	x	3	x	3	=	36
/		x		+		+		
7	+	3	/	5	+	4	=	6
x		/		/		x		
8	-	6	+	8	+	3	=	13
-		+		+		+		
10	+	7	-	9	+	9	=	17
=		=		=		=		
6		12		10		30		

4.3.6.

34	+	8	/	7	/	3	=	2
/		x		+		+		
17	-	2	/	5	+	11	=	14
+		/		+		+		
7	x	4	-	20	x	3	=	24
/		+		/		-		
3	+	5	+	8	/	2	=	8
=		=		=		=		
3		9		4		15		

4.3.7.

12	/	6	x	15	-	8	=	22
+		+		+		+		
7	+	3	/	5	+	5	=	7
-		/		/		+		
4	x	3	-	4	x	3	=	24
/		-		x		/		
5	x	2	+	6	/	2	=	8
=		=		=		=		
3		1		30		8		

4.3.8.

40	/	10	x	3	+	3	=	15
/		+		/		+		
8	/	4	+	1	+	10	=	13
x		/		x		+		
3	+	7	x	5	-	17	=	33
-		+		+		/		
5	+	9	x	2	-	15	=	13
=		=		=		=		
10		11		17		2		

4.3.9.

19	+	6	/	5	-	3	=	2
x		+		+		+		
3	+	4	-	6	x	3	=	3
-		+		+		+		
27	/	3	+	1	/	5	=	2
/		+		/		-		
10	x	3	-	2	/	7	=	4
=		=		=		=		
3		16		6		4		

4.3.10.

13	+	12	/	5	-	1	=	4
-		/		+		+		
10	-	4	x	3	-	5	=	13
x		+		+		x		
5	-	3	x	7	+	5	=	19
+		/		/		-		
4	+	2	+	5	+	17	=	28
=		=		=		=		
19		3		3		13		

4.3.11.

13	-	3	x	3	-	4	=	26
-		+		x		+		
7	+	8	+	3	+	5	=	23
/		+		+		x		
2	+	13	/	5	+	5	=	8
x		/		/		-		
9	+	12	/	7	+	7	=	10
=		=		=		=		
27		2		2		38		

4.3.12.

9	+	12	/	3	-	4	=	3
-		-		+		+		
8	+	8	-	6	+	9	=	19
x		x		/		+		
16	+	9	-	3	-	5	=	17
/		-		+		-		
4	+	15	+	5	/	8	=	3
=		=		=		=		
4		21		8		10		

4.3.13.

39	/	3	+	11	/	12	=	2
-		+		+		/		
17	+	11	-	6	+	6	=	28
/		-		+		x		
2	+	9	+	3	-	13	=	1
+		x		/		-		
3	+	5	/	4	x	6	=	12
=		=		=		=		
14		25		5		20		

4.3.14.

49	/	7	-	4	x	12	=	36
+		+		+		+		
11	-	9	+	11	+	6	=	19
/		/		/		/		
15	+	8	+	3	/	2	=	13
+		+		+		x		
7	+	4	+	10	/	7	=	3
=		=		=		=		
11		6		15		63		

4.3.15.

40	/	8	-	4	+	18	=	19
-		+		x		/		
20	-	11	/	3	x	6	=	18
+		-		+		+		
10	+	1	+	5	/	4	=	4
/		/		+		x		
15	-	3	+	6	/	2	=	9
=		=		=		=		
2		6		23		14		

4.3.16.

13	x	2	-	5	-	13	=	8
+		+		+		+		
7	+	11	/	6	+	7	=	10
/		-		-		.+		
4	+	12	/	8	+	7	=	9
x		+		+		/		
5	+	14	+	5	-	9	=	15
=		=		=		=		
25		15		8		3		

4.3.17.

36	-	19	+	3	/	5	=	4
/		-		+		x		
4	+	4	+	27	-	6	=	29
+		+		-		-		
5	+	8	-	7	+	5	=	11
/		+		-		/		
7	+	3	/	10	+	5	=	6
=		=		=		=		
2		26		13		5		

4.3.18.

16	+	12	/	14	x	9	=	18
+		-		+		+		
35	/	5	+	12	-	3	=	16
/		+		/		-		
3	+	7	/	2	+	8	=	13
-		/		-		+		
4	+	7	+	4	/	3	=	5
=		=		=		=		
13		2		9		7		

4.3.19.

4	+	3	+	15	-	13	=	9
+		-		/		+		
8	+	1	/	3	+	17	=	20
/		+		+		/		
12	-	8	+	6	/	5	=	2
+		/		-		-		
38	/	2	-	4	+	5	=	20
=		=		=		=		
39		5		7		1		

4.3.20.

39	+	1	/	5	/	2	=	4
/		+		x		x		
13	+	6	-	1	/	6	=	3
x		x		+		+		
4	+	7	+	2	-	6	=	7
-		-		+		+		
5	+	13	x	3	-	1	=	53
=		=		=		=		
7		36		10		19		

5.1. Steffi was alone in the apartment from 11:00am to 11:15am. She had to be careful not to be seen by the carriers, when they shortly put down the pieces of furniture.
5.2. Tim has to call at 5:00am.
5.3. Hint 1: Pay attention to the 15 minute walk from the lake/boat house and the house/barn.
Hint 2: Mr. Schmidt could not have been murdered until 16:15pm, as a group has still been in his room at 16:00pm. Since the body has not been moved after death and the room looked normal, he could not have been dead at that time. Kai Fischer is the offender. When Steffen Reif left him at the boathouse at 19:30pm, he was alone. Till 20:00pm, he had time to walk back to the house and commit the crime. He had even a few minutes longer, so that he could prepare the crime scene, since the food began not until 20:15pm.
5.4.

age	youngest			eldest
holiday	most		less	
size		tallest		smallest
weight		heaviest	light weightiest	
children	2	none	most	less

5.5. Hint 1: Johann´s conclusion that the key is missing at 23:30pm makes no difference. The offender may have stolen it sometime earlier and also may have driven the motorcycle later.
Hint 2: Johann did not arrive before 21:00pm. No one could have stolen the motorcycle previously.
Maik had no alibi between 2:30am and 3:30am. He is the only guest who was not found in any group for an hour at that time. He is the offender.

5.6.

	person 1	person2	person3	person4	person5
alcohol	X	**X**			
smoking	X		X	X	
car racing		**X**	X		
soccer				X	X
sports					X
candy		**X**			

Those things are alcohol, car racing and candy.

5.7.

	1	2	3	4	5	6
spaghetti	yes		yes			no
coffee	yes		no		yes	
pork		no		no		yes
fish	**no**	yes		yes		
wine	**no**		yes		no	yes
pineapple	**no**	yes	yes	yes	yes	no
curd	yes	no		no		

5.8.

The man is faster without moving walkway than with moving walkway.
Sample calculation:
Constant speed: 100m in 3 minutes
The results with moving walkway:
One way (forth): 100m in 1min 30sec.
Way back (return): 100m in 6 min.
Without moving walkway:
One way (forth): 3 min
Way back (return): 3 min
In this example, it takes the man 6 minutes without moving walkway and 7.5 minutes with moving walkway.

5.9. Rolf and Barbara cannot have done it. They have no motive to fake a burglary. Stephanie and Frank have met each other recently and therefore, it can be excluded that both commit such a crime immediately. However, Maik and Susi have not been seen from 18:30pm to 19:30pm. They were the only ones who had time for the offense.

5.10.
(Bernd is 15 years younger than Wolfgang and he will be half his age in 4 years)

Bernd: 11 years
Wolfgang: 26 years
(Tom+ Bettina= 33 years(+7 of Wolfgang). Tom is 7 years older than Bettina)
Tom: 20 years
Bettina: 13 years
(4 years ago, Maik was as old as Bettina will be in 15 years)
Bettina in 15 years and Maik 4 years ago: 28 years old
Maik (today): 32 years
(Gothold = Maik(32)+Tom(20)+Bettina(13)=65)
Gothold: 65 years
(Steffi + Wolfgang(26) + Bernd(11) =69 Gothold in 4 years)
Steffi: 32 years
(Susi+Tina+Marike=32(Steffi) Susi and Tina have the same age. Marike is 4 years younger than Steffi)
Susi/Tina: 12 years
Marike: 8 years

5.11.
First trip: 2 tigers to the new shore
First return trip: 1 Tiger back to the old shore
Second trip: 2 tigers to the new shore
Second return trip: 1 Tiger to the old shore
Third trip: 2 Zebras to the new shore
Third return trip: 1 Tiger and 1 Zebra to the old shore
Fourth trip: 2 Zebras to the new shore
Fourth return trip: 1 Tiger to the old shore
Fifth trip: 2 tigers to the new shore
Fifth return trip: 1 Tiger to the old shore
Last trip: 2 tigers to the new shore

5.12.
Hint 1: Jürgen and Christine provide the entry.
Hint 2: In Christine's statement about the number of all employees, she is not included. The current number cannot be determined by her, since the period between the 5th year and today is not known.

	today	5th year	3th year	foundation
Michael	22			
Gunther	22		22	11
Jürgen	**15**	14	15	9
Christine	FREE	7	5	2
Kerstin	8		12	
Heike	8			

5.13.

stars		■	■	■	■	■				■	■	■	■		
flowers						■	■	■	■		■	■	■		
circles	■				■	■	■	■							
squares					■	■	■	■		■	■	■	■		
lines	■		■		■										
waves			■				■								
figures							■	■	■			■			
houses					■										
animals	■	■	■												
ring	■														

Question 1:
There are exactly 2 cups which represent 6 pattern. (stars, flowers, squares, waves, houses and the bottom ring)
Question 2:
There are 5 cups which only have the circle at the bottom.

5.14.
Hint: At the beginning, look at Tina, Gabi and Susi.
Solution (Tina, Gabi, Susi):
Tina+Gabi=750€
Tina: 750€/2+100€
Gabi: 750€/2-100€
Susi: 750€/2
After that, everything is easy to follow up. Maria, Nicole and Martina remain. Set some formulae.
Variables: Maria: V / Nicole: C / Martina: T
V+C+T=720
V=C/2+35
C=2V-70
T=C+V-100
Rearrange the formulae:
-100=T-C-V
720=V+C+T
Simplify the formulae:
620=2T
T=310

Tina: 475€
Gabi: 275€
Susi: 375€
Katrin: 130€
Anna: 120€
Doreen: 360€
Steffi: 180€
Sophia: 90€ (Question 1)
Maria: 160€
Nicole: 250€
Martina: 310€ (Question 2)

5.15. The person is wearing a white shirt.

1st person	2nd person	3th person	4th person
yellow jacket	red pants	**white shirt**	black shoes
pay cash	debit	credit card	on credit
2 products	3 products	5 products	10 products
meat	fruit	cheese	drinks

6.1.
Column 3 and 7.

6.2.
Note at the beginning: The fourth column and the third row of the table. If each number exists only once, and the neighbors are only 1 apart, it can only be a simple counting sequence. Since the third row (second number of column) only has even numbers, the count can only go in one direction. Namely, from top to bottom. Otherwise, 5 would be at this point.

2	5	1	3	4	6
4	4	2	2	6	6
3	5	3	1	3	5
1	6	4	2	3	5
4	5	5	3	3	6
3	4	6	2	1	5

6.3.
The solution´s order may vary. Correlations result from the same summands, factors of rows and columns. Procedures can be deduced from other blocks in the same row/column.
Hint 1: The first line in the second and third block can be solved first.

Hint 2: Then, the second column of the first, third and fourth block is also solvable.
Hint 3: The fourth column of the third and fourth block can be solved.
Hint 4: The first column of the first, second and fourth block can be solved.
Hint 5: The last number (fourth row, fourth block) can be determined by summation.

1	2	3	4
6	4	4	3
11	8	1	2
16	16	58	1

3	4	5	6
7	8	1	5
11	16	5	4
15	32	15	3

5	6	7	8
8	12	1	7
11	24	1	6
14	48	-23	5

7	8	9	10
9	16	14	9
11	32	11	8
13	64	-88	7

6.4.
1. All birds are warm-blooded animals. This is true, but the text says that mammals are warm-blooded animals, and birds do not belong to mammals.
2. All birds are not fish. These animal species are faced nowhere, not even indirectly.
3. Some fish suckle their young. That mammals suckle their young is absolutely right. However, this is not stated in the text.
4. Birds do not hibernate. Although, this is correct. But the text only says that mammals do not hibernate.
5. Some carnivores are not cats. Correct. This answer is correct.
6. Some amphibians are not carnivores. It is only said that frogs are amphibians and carnivores. Thus, since frogs are a subset of amphibians, nothing can be said about the entire genus.

6.5.
Hint 1: In each square there is a certain number of geometrical figures.
Hint 2: The arithmetic operators can also point to a series.
Solution:
The first 3 numbers are positive and then a negative number follows. In the continuation, three positive numbers are searched again. Because nothing else is pointed out, you can conclude that the series starts again from the beginning. The question is now, how to get the numbers. In the first square there are 3 lines. In the second square there are 4 circles, in the third square there are 3 triangles and in the fourth one there is an arrow. Since the series restarts, the solution is as follows:
First number: 2 (2 lines)
Second number: 2 (2 circles)
Third number: 1 (1 triangle)
Result: 14

6.6.
Hint 1: There are 4 different symbols.
Hint 2: To get letters for the words, you have to deduce a number from each symbol.
Hint 3: The number of symbols is important.
Result:
Square: 23 (W)
Triangle: 9 (I)
Star: 5 (E)
Arrow: 14 (N)
Result: Wien: The German word for Vienna.

6.7.
The solution fields have a uniform marking.

4	+	11	+	18	=	33
+		-		+		
16	+	1	-	6	=	11
/		/		-		
5	*	5	-	19	=	6
=		=		=		
4	+	10	-	5	=	9

16 = P / 1 = A / 18 = R / 9 = I / 19 = S
In the correct order: Paris

6.8. The beam flies from the perspective of the orange spaceship with around 300,000 km/s.

This riddle rather is a knowledge riddle than a logic riddle. In the theory of relativity, for the first time, the strange fact was shown that light, independent of the observer, always has the same speed. Thus, the beam of each of the 9 spaceships is equally fast, namely about 300,000 km/s. This phenomenon is known as "time dilation".

6.9.
The mother was dismissed at the age of 40. (The father of Markus and Sophia is 58 years. The calculation is quite simple up to that. 15 years ago, his wife was 29 years old. Therefore, she is now 44 and was dismissed 4 years ago.)